CW00821328

Guide to Supply Chain Management

Colin Scott · Henriette Lundgren ·
Paul Thompson

Guide to
Supply Chain Management

 Springer

Colin Scott
Grange Partnership (UK) LLP
The Grange, Elmbridge
WR9 0DA Droitwich
United Kingdom
colin.scott@grangepartnership.com

Henriette Lundgren
Grange Partnership (UK) LLP
The Grange, Elmbridge
WR9 0DA Droitwich
United Kingdom
henriette.lundgren@grangepartnership.com

Paul Thompson
Grange Partnership (UK) LLP
The Grange, Elmbridge
WR9 0DA Droitwich
United Kingdom
paul.thompson@grangepartnership.com

ISBN 978-3-642-17675-3   e-ISBN 978-3-642-17676-0
DOI 10.1007/978-3-642-17676-0
Springer Heidelberg Dordrecht London New York

Library of Congress Control Number: 2011923331

Cover design: WMXDesign GmbH, Heidelberg, Germany

Printed on acid-free paper

Springer is part of Springer Science+Business Media (www.springer.com)

Acknowledgement

We'd like to acknowledge and thank our families and everyone who supported us in this project, particularly on the text and case studies.

Foreword

This guide is a really useful reminder of what good practice is and how it should be applied within supply chain management. The book is relevant for students of supply chain management and professional practitioners alike.

The key aspects of supply chain are laid out clearly – plan, source, make, deliver, and return. The book is well constructed in totality – and I can envisage revisiting specific chapters in isolation whilst constructing and delivering supply chain strategy.

This is the first book that I have come across that is focussed more upon the concepts underpinning the total supply chain rather than the physical execution of the supply chain. Its range is from forecasting, inventory management and cash through execution strategy and development. I would add it to my arsenal and recommend it to others.

The content is relevant; concepts are clearly explained and supported by case studies that bring the concepts to life. The language used is clear and contemporary, visualisations re-enforce the concepts well. The additional suggested reading at the end of each chapter offers an added opportunity to further develop understanding of specific elements of the supply chain.

Organisations operating on a global stage have to get this stuff right, both in process and physical terms: it is an essential element to delivering profitable growth. This book offers an invaluable guide to understanding the specific dynamics of your supply chain and the fundamentals underpinning it. It provides the framework for delivering a supply chain strategy based upon recognised best practice.

Chief Executive Officer   Martin McCourt
Dyson Limited
Wiltshire, Uk

Preface

Supply chain management is a fast-growing business. Over the last ten years, it has driven companies around the world to change structure and – maybe more importantly – the way they think about operating in a global environment. Everything we consume from the food we eat and the clothes we wear, to the cars we drive, is configured from components that have travelled from different corners of the world. As consumers request high-quality products at lower cost, supply chain management has become as critical as sales, marketing and finance in today's organisations.

Companies that produce and move products are finding it more and more difficult to make themselves unique or different from the competition, where success is evermore difficult to achieve. As a consequence, releasing opportunities in supply chains is now, as ever, the goal to beat competition – and provide better service at lower cost.

During our work as supply chain trainers for large multinational companies in various industries we have met professionals all over the world who are passionate about achieving these goals. This guide is designed to help professionals, students and everyone else with an interest in this topic to structure their thoughts and methodologies.

Business practitioners who work in supply chain management and those whose business functions interact with it will also have an interest in reading the guide. Students, whether studying at universities or in vocational training, will find this guide a comprehensive introduction to supply chain management. But also people working in other contexts, such as charity projects or professional industry bodies will find this text useful with its intuitive models and many practical examples.

In writing this guide, we have tried to connect with our readers by using simple and straightforward models. By including real-life examples and case studies of best practice, the guide aims to bring supply chain theory to life. The practical approach and format will enable readers to capitalise on the insights presented in the guide.

In preparing this book, we have drawn greatly on the thoughts and concepts of others. If we have omitted to give any credits where credits are due, we apologise and hope that they will make contact to include in future editions. Learning is an interactive experience, so we welcome any feedback or ideas of how to improve this guide. After all, we have learned most from the people we worked with.

If you would like to get in touch with the authors, please email us: feedback@ grangepartnership.com

Worcestershire, UK   Colin Scott
                                                                          Henriette Lundgren
                                                                             Paul Thompson

Contents

Abbreviations

3PL	3rd party logistics
AS	Average stockholding
B2B	Business to business
B2C	Business to consumer
CFO	Chief financial officer
CILT	Chartered Institute of Logistics and Transportation
CLSC	Closed loop supply chain
COC	Cost of capital
COFC	Container on flat car
COG	Centre of gravity
CRP	Capacity requirements planning
CS	Category sourcing
CSR	Corporate social responsibility
DC	Distribution centre
DRP	Distribution requirements planning
ELV	End of life vehicle
EOQ	Economic order quantity
EPA	Environmental Protection Agency
FA	Forecast accuracy
FE	Forecast error
FG	Finished goods
FMCG	Fast moving consumer goods
FTL	Full truck load
GSCM	Green supply chain management
HAZMAT	Hazardous material
IP	Intellectual property
ITT	Invitation to tender
JIT	Just in time
KPI	Key performance indicators
L&D	Learning & development
LNG	Liquid natural gas

LT	Lead-time
LTL	Less than a truck load
MAPE	Mean absolute percentage error
MPS	Master production schedule
MRP	Materials requirements planning
NDC	National Distribution Centre
NLP	Neuro-linguistic programming
NVA	Non-value added
OAM	Original equipment manufacture
OOS	Out of stock
OTIF	On time in full
P&L	Profit & loss
Q	Order quantity
R&D	Research & Development
RCCP	Rough cut capacity planning
RDC	Regional distribution centre
RFI	Request for information
RFP	Request for proposal
RFQ	Request for quotation
RL	Reverse logistics
RM	Raw materials
ROCE	Return on capital employed
RRT	Rolling road train
S&OP	Sales & operations planning
SC	Supply chain
SCC	Supply chain council
SCM	Supply chain management
SCOR	Supply chain operations reference
SKU	Stock keeping unit
SLA	Service level agreement
SLF	Service level factor
SRM	Supplier relationship management
SS	Safety stock
SU	Supplier uncertainty
TCO	Total cost of ownership
TOC	Theory of constraints
TOFC	Trailer on flat car
TPS	Toyota production system
TQM	Total quality management
ULD	Unit load device
VARK	Visual, auditory, read/write, kinaesthetic
WACC	Weighted average cost of capital
WEEE	Waste electrical and electronic equipment
WIP	Work in progress

Chapter 1
Introduction to Supply Chain Management

Abstract This chapter guides you through the basics of supply chain management. First, it introduces you to a supply chain with simple product, information and fund flows. Second, it outlines a functional view on supply chain management and the structure of the following five chapters on plan, source, make, deliver and return will be introduced. Third, it will look at the supply chain players and dynamics. Here you will be introduced to the challenge of balancing supply and demand with inventory. The chapter closes with a brief introduction to the next ten chapters on supply chain management.

Having read this chapter you will be able to:

- Clarify what supply chains are and name their main components
- Define a recommended functional model to categorise supply chain processes
- Determine the players and dynamics in product supply chains

1.1 What Starts a Supply Chain?

Whether you are a tea or coffee drinker – have you ever wondered how your hot drink makes its way onto your breakfast table? Have a look at the supply chain diagram in Fig. 1.1. What do you see?

Firstly, let's consider the flow of materials – these are depicted in the middle part of the diagram. They range from raw materials (tea leaves), to work in progress (silo), all the way to finished goods (a cup of tea). This goods flow encompasses the supplier's supplier through to end consumer.

Secondly, we have the flow of information, e.g. order confirmation or dispatch advice.

In addition, there are also reverse flows. These reverse flows can be in the form of:

- Goods, e.g. quality defect products or obsolete products
- Information, e.g. customer feedback
- Packaging material, e.g. outer cartons
- Transportation equipment, e.g. cages, pallets or containers

C. Scott et al., *Guide to Supply Chain Management*,
DOI 10.1007/978-3-642-17676-0_1, © Springer-Verlag Berlin Heidelberg 2011

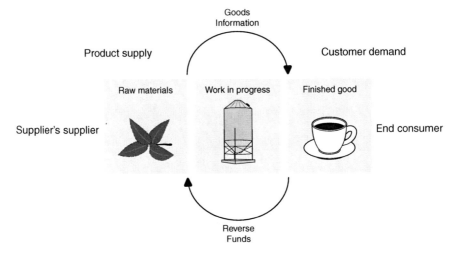

Fig. 1.1 The supply chain of a cup of tea

We also have the reverse flow of funds. This is the money that flows back into the supply chain. Ultimately, the supplier's supplier wants to be paid for the delivery of tea leaves!

Thus, tracking your breakfast drink all the way back from its source of raw materials shows a number of players and processes involved.

Figure 1.1 also depicts two forces in this chain of goods, information and funds:

1. Product supply
2. Customer demand

Which of these two starts the supply chain?

Imagine a scenario where a retail outlet is operating from *customer demand*. You enter as a consumer with the intention to buy some tea bags. You find the tea and coffee shelf empty. Instead of the full assortment of black, green, fruit and herbal tea, there is a sign over the counter saying, "Please order your favourite tea here". Irritated by the absence of *product supply* you would probably go and see the shop assistant for clarification. They would then explain to you that the shop is running a *customer demand* driven tea supply chain where the end consumer can place an order directly in the shop. The order is then automatically transmitted to the tea bag supplier in India in order to grow, pick and process the required amount of tea leaves that are filled into tea bags. Does that work?

It probably does not. Commodities, such as tea, coffee, rice, bread, milk and most other basic consumer products that you find in supermarkets are more likely to be produced on a *product supply* basis. This means that the supply chain starts supplying before you come into the supermarket to buy some tea bags. As a consequence, you find supermarket shelves full of products for everyday use. The same applies to small household equipment, electronics and general fashion clothes – mostly these are sourced, produced and shipped in advance. So in this case, *product supply* starts the supply chain.

Unlike tea bags, some products are produced based on *customer demand*. These products are typically characterised by a high degree of customisation. Here, the customer order starts the chain of supply, manufacturing and transport activities of your desired product. Some typical products of *customer demand* driven products are: tailor-made clothes, customised tools and dinner in an up-market fish restaurant. Here customers see the fish that they are going to eat later on still swimming in the fish tank when they enter the restaurant. The chain starts moving after you have expressed your wish or after you have set your order. Thus, the supply chain starts with *customer demand*.

To summarise, supply chains can be triggered by product supply (commodities) or by customer demand (customised products). The degree of customisation dictates how much and in which format the supplying company holds inventory: no stock at all, raw or basic materials only or sub-assemblies of their products as in the famous example of Dell computers. The strategies and associated decoupling of product supply from customer demand form a crucial part of supply chain management (see Chap. 7 on Strategy).

1.2 A Functional View of Supply Chain Management

In order to understand the supply chain better, it makes sense to break it down into functional processes. The Supply Chain Council (SCC), an industry body representing supply chain companies and industry players, has developed the Supply Chain Operations Reference (SCOR) model that depicts the broad spectrum of generic functional processes in the supply chain (see Fig. 1.2).

Let's go back to our first example in this chapter: the tea bag supply chain. Imagine that you are the manufacturer of these tea bags. When you start engaging in

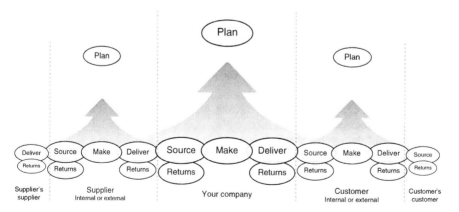

Fig. 1.2 The supply chain operations reference model
Source: http://www.supply-chain.org, SCOR model, Supply Chain Council Inc, Copyright © 2010

supply chain management, you will most likely be confronted with some of these questions:

- How many tea bags are you going to sell?
- Where are you going to sell them and when?
- How much production do you need to schedule in your factory?
- What are your raw and packaging materials you need in order to fulfil the production plan?

All of these belong to the functional *plan* process, where demand and supply are balanced to develop a course of action to meet sourcing, production and delivery needs. The plan process aligns the supply chain plan with the financial plan (see Chap. 2 on Plan).

The next step is to find suppliers of tea leaves, tea bag sachets and outer packaging cartons in order to source your materials that you need for production. You might also decide to source services such as transport and warehousing. This *source* function is sometimes called purchasing or procurement, and it describes the process of buying goods or services to meet planned or actual demand. The emphasis in this stage of the process is on selecting suppliers, establishing policies and assessing performance (see Chap. 3 on Source).

Once demand and supply are planned, and materials are sourced, you can start with the actual manufacturing or making of tea bags. Thus, the header *make* in this model describes all processes that transform your raw materials or sub-assemblies into the finished product with the aim to meet customer demand. This process within the supply chain operations reference model looks at questions such as:

- How to set up manufacturing?
- How to make sure the production runs efficiently?
- How to improve the making process? (see Chap. 4 on Make)

After manufacturing, your products are ready for distribution or delivery. Under the *deliver* function, all supply chain processes are included that provide finished goods to customers. Thus, the order management, warehousing and transport management of your tea bags all form part of this process (see Chap. 5 on Deliver).

The last process in the chain concerns reverse logistics or product *return*. This functional process comprises all tasks that are associated with the return of product. Returns can occur for quality reasons, for recycling or for post delivery customer support (see Chap. 6 on Return).

The supply chain operations reference model furthermore shows that these functional processes of plan, source, make, deliver and return take place within every stage of the supply chain.

1.3 Supply Chain Players

Let's now have a look at the different supply chain players. In its simplest format, a supply chain consists of three players. The company, e.g. the producer of tea bags, the supplier, e.g. local companies that produce raw and packaging materials, and the customer of that company, e.g. local supermarkets as demonstrated in the following example (see Fig. 1.3).

In an extended supply chain, we consider three additional supply chain players. On the upstream side (towards supply), there is the supplier's supplier or the ultimate supplier at the beginning of the extended chain. In our tea bag example, it could be the cotton farmer in Texas who provides the raw material for the supplier to produce tea bag sachets. At the downstream side (towards demand), there is the customer's customer or the end consumer at the end of the extended supply chain. The distinction here is the different kind of customers that exist between your company and the end consumer.

Customers in supply chains can be distributors, wholesalers or retailers. Distributors are companies that take inventory in bulk from manufacturers and deliver an assortment of related product lines to customers. Distributors are common in regions where retailing is fragmented, e.g. in some parts of Latin America, and for certain channels of distribution, e.g. petrol stations and airports. Wholesalers – often known as cash & carry markets – buy from distributors or manufacturers directly. They often specialise in certain product ranges and supply special industries, like hotels, restaurants and catering, with larger quantities of products. Retailers, on the other hand, stock products in smaller quantities and sell them to the general public. These are the different kinds of customers in a product supply chain.

In this guide, we will sometimes refer to supply chain or product companies. These are companies that sit in the middle of the chain – just like in the example of the simple or extended supply chains – and bring products to market together with their supply chain partners.

Finally, there are entire categories of companies that are service providers to other players in the supply chain. These perform services in areas such as:

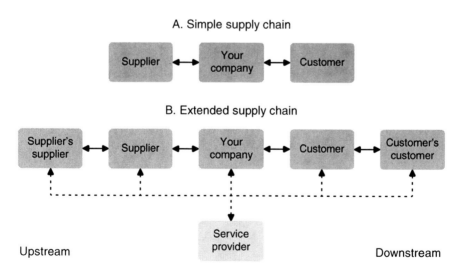

Fig. 1.3 Supply chain structures

- Transportation
- Warehousing
- Finance
- Market research
- New product design
- Information, communication and technology

Service providers specialise in certain skills and expertise. They are often able to provide these services more efficiently than manufacturers, distributors, wholesalers, retailers or end consumers.

Supply chain structures, however, may have many more players involved if you look at them from the very beginning until the very end. Drawing your own or your customer's supply chain can help you to understand the supply chain dynamics better.

When you look at your finished supply chain map, you probably find multiple upstream and downstream players including some of service providers. You could further ask yourself:

- What's the geography of my supply chain map?
- What happens when a flow is interrupted?
- Who pays for the cost of inefficient supply chains?

1.4 Supply Chain Dynamics

Though their set-up often appears to be static, supply chains in reality are quite dynamic. Ideally, supply chains react to changes in their environment. Maybe it helps to draw another picture to illustrate this point. A supply chain can be compared to a huge water reservoir, like the Hoover Dam close to Las Vegas (see Fig. 1.4): it reacts to how much water is needed in a given period (rate of customer

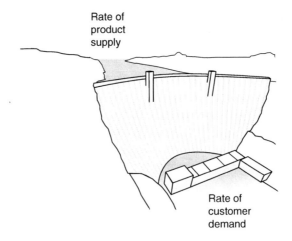

Fig. 1.4 Balancing supply and demand

demand) and opens its reservoir accordingly (rate of product supply). It is important that the rate of supply mirrors the rate of demand; otherwise the outcome will be very unfavourable for Las Vegas.

The same is true for players in the supply chain. Their task is to balance the rate of product supply in accordance with the rate of customer demand. This is, as practitioners of supply chains will know, very difficult at times. External influences will affect the equilibrium. The demand for ice cream, for example, depends on how hot it is during the summer. Price cuts and promotional activities will influence the sale of cars. Other macroeconomic factors such as exchange rates, affect world travel and consumption. Yet, it is useful to keep the water reservoir image in mind when working in supply chains.

Managing supply chains can feel at times like surfing. It is constant rolling, riding and gliding on and off the waves (see Fig. 1.5).

As a surfer, you are aiming to stay on top of the wave! In supply chains, the wave stands for inventory and you are constantly managing the level of inventory against the risk of being out of stock. You may decide to increase your level of inventory and therefore reduce the level of stock outs. This situation feels comfortable as long as your Finance Director does not push for a reduction in working capital and higher returns on capital employed (see Chap. 9 on Finance). Thus, inventory reduction might become necessary despite being paired with an increased risk of out of stocks. The challenge in supply chain management is to balance the level of inventory while maintaining a high level of service (see Chap. 10 on Customer Service).

A famous simulation of dynamics in the supply chain is the *beer game*. The set-up is simple: there are four players (factory, distributor, wholesaler and retailer) that source, produce and move beer within the supply chain. The aim is to minimise total supply chain costs, which can be achieved through holding little (but not too little!) inventory. Then it happens: the bullwhip effect! A small change in real customer demand leads to a huge amplification of the upstream demand signal and increased volatility of orders through to suppliers. The initial out of stock situation soon becomes a massive excess stock problem. In order to improve the situation, we

Fig. 1.5 The inventory challenge

need to communicate, share a demand forecast between the different players and reduce information and product flow lead-times.

In addition to those just mentioned, there are more learning points from the *beer game* that lead to best practice in supply chain management. The human factor, for example, becomes highly important in supply chain performance. Silo thinking (thinking in isolation) needs to be avoided and a lack of supply chain understanding needs to be addressed (see Chap. 8 on People). Also, loss of control, lack of service and frequent quality problems can be the consequence when dealing with many players in the supply chain. Therefore, the management of partners in the supply chain, e.g. third party logistics providers, becomes crucial (see Chap. 11 on Outsourcing).

The first part of this book will guide you through the functional processes of the supply chain operations reference model (Chaps. 2–6), whilst the second part (Chaps. 7–11) is dedicated to strategic questions of supply chain management. Each chapter builds up in an easy way: first, the chapter topic is introduced. The chapter continues with an explanation why the topic is important in the context of supply chain management. Next, practical tools for improvement will be given. Finally each chapter concludes with a case study of best practices from companies around the globe.

You will find some suggestions for further reading at the end of each chapter.

Chapter 2
Guide to Plan in Supply Chain Management

Abstract This chapter guides you through the planning function of supply chain management. First, it helps you to understand inventory management within supply chains and gives you practical ways on how to reduce stock. Second, demand planning including forecasting techniques will be discussed. This leads to supply planning where different inventory review strategies and the economic order quantity will be introduced. Third, demand and supply planning will be reconciled in the section of sales and operations planning. In this section, both guiding principles of successful implementations and reasons for failure will be described. The chapter concludes with a case study of best practice on forecasting within the skin and beauty care company Beiersdorf.

Having read this chapter you will be able to:

- Clarify the basics of inventory management
- Explore the link between demand and supply planning
- Recognise the guiding principles of successful sales & operations planning

2.1 Inventory and Supply Chains

The term inventory can be defined as the quantity of goods that is available on hand or in stock. There are three main formats of inventory: raw material, work in progress and finished goods. These depict the different product stages on a continuum from product supply to customer demand. In order to understand the role of inventory in the supply chain it may be sensible to ask the question: Why hold inventory? There may be several answers (see Fig. 2.1).

First and foremost, inventory is held to *protect against uncertainty*. Uncertainty can be caused by variations in demand or by restrictions in supply. We will go into more detail when we talk about safety stock later in this chapter.

Cost reduction through inventory is achieved when stock is held close to the customer. IKEA for example holds their furniture in stores so that customers can pay for their products and immediately take them home. IKEA thus minimises its transportation cost to customers.

C. Scott et al., *Guide to Supply Chain Management*,
DOI 10.1007/978-3-642-17676-0_2, © Springer-Verlag Berlin Heidelberg 2011

Fig. 2.1 Reasons for holding inventory

Another important reason for holding inventory is to *protect against quality defects*. A product that is faulty can be substituted quickly when inventory is held. If there was no inventory in the supply chain and a product was damaged on the way to its customer, the customer would have to wait a long time until a substitute was available.

Inventory can also be used to *stabilise manufacturing*. For example, the demand for ice cream increases substantially in the summer. To be able to meet this demand, ice cream is produced throughout the year and kept in stock. This approach, which can be seen in the production of many seasonal items, is especially important where manufacturing technology is expensive and therefore needs to be utilised throughout the year in order to get a good return on investment.

Anticipation stock is similar to the example just mentioned. However, the reason for this sort of inventory is rather demand than supply driven. Before the launch of a product innovation like the iPhone, for which the level and rate of demand was fairly unknown, Apple Inc. might have decided to build up pre-launch anticipation stock to buffer against demand uncertainty.

To summarise, managing inventory is essentially about *balancing supply and demand*. This job would be very easy in a situation where end customers tell us exactly how much they require and give us time to order from suppliers. Also, ideally suppliers deliver exactly when we need it and in full. If these three conditions were true, we wouldn't need a buffer but could order from a supplier and ship it on to customers in time to satisfy their need.

2.1.1 Different Types of Inventory

Now that we have understood the necessity of holding inventory, let's distinguish between several different types of inventory:

- Cycle or replenishment stock: This stock keeps the supply chain moving. Cycle stock is the inventory necessary to meet the normal daily demand.
- Safety stock: This stock buffers against forecast error and the supplier's unreliability.
- In-transit stock: This stock is in the process of being transported to a stocking or delivery point.
- Seasonal stock: This stock is built up in advance to meet increased sales volumes during a particular time of the year.
- Promotional stock: This stock feeds into marketing campaigns and advertising.
- Speculative stock: This stock is held to protect against price increases or periods of limited availability.
- Dead or obsolete stock: This stock is no longer usable or saleable in the market.

Although all types of inventory are important, cycle stock and safety stock are those types that are most looked after in inventory management. We will therefore discuss these two types of stock in more detail in the next sections.

2.1.2 Cycle Stock

In order to understand the concept of cycle stock, let's look at a simple example. A fruit vendor operates out of Majorca and sells oranges. The business is small and sales are constant: the fruit vendor sells just one orange every day of the week. The vendor sources oranges from a local fruit supplier who delivers once a week on Monday morning to the small shop in Majorca (see Fig. 2.2)

	Delivery	Sales	Cycle Stock
Monday	7	1	6
Tuesday	-	1	5
Wednesday	-	1	4
Thursday	-	1	3
Friday	-	1	2
Saturday	-	1	1
Sunday	-	1	0
Total	7	7	-

Fig. 2.2 Cycle stock example

Thus, the amount of seven oranges that the fruit man gets delivered every week on Monday morning into stock is called cycle stock.

When talking about cycle stock, it is worthwhile looking at how much stock we hold throughout the year. The average stock holding calculation is based on the order quantity. In the example above, the stock holding was highest on Monday morning when he had just received the weekly delivery. It was lowest on Sunday evening when all stock had been sold. Therefore, as the level of stock varies between the maximum at the time of receipt and the minimum just before the next delivery, we can define the average stockholding as:

$$AS = \frac{Q}{2} \tag{2.1}$$

where AS = average stockholding and Q = order quantity

Let's consider another example. An electronics retailer annually sells 400 Plasma TV's, orders once a year and receives one delivery per year. In this example average stock holding can be determined as

$$400/2 = 200$$

The average stock holding can also be depicted graphically (see Fig. 2.3).

From the average cycle stock holding quantity, we can derive the average cycle stock investment taking into consideration the product price of one unit of stock. Let's assume that one TV costs €5,000. Then the average cycle stock investment would equal average stockholding multiplied by the cost of one TV, thus:

$$200 \times €5,000 = €1,000,000.$$

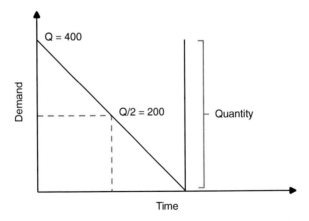

Fig. 2.3 Cycle stock – average stock holding

One million Euros of average capital investment might be quite a stretch for a small electronics retailer. Instead of ordering once a year, the electronics retailer could order twice a year and thus reduce its cycle stock investment. By ordering more often the average inventory costs would now be

$$200/2 \times €5,000 = €500,000.$$

2.1.3 Safety Stock

We have just explored the concept of cycle stock and average cycle stock investment. Safety stock is different from cycle stock as it does not cover the regular rate of sales but protects against uncertainty.

To understand the concept of safety stock, let's revisit the fruit vendor in Majorca. He still sells one orange per day, seven oranges a week and receives one weekly delivery of seven oranges on Monday morning. But then one week something unexpected happens. The fruit supplier does not show up on Monday morning, or on Tuesday morning, but only on Wednesday morning. The vendor is angry with his supplier since he had an out-of-stock (OOS) of oranges for 2 days. As a consequence, he decides to order more oranges – exactly two more – to protect himself from the fruit supplier coming 2 days late again. These extra two oranges can be considered as safety stock as they are meant to protect the fruit man against the uncertainty of the supplier coming late.

There is a more elaborate way to estimate safety stock. In fact, there are two parts of the equation to account for in the safety stock calculation:

(a) Safety stock supply that covers unplanned production and delivery delays
(b) Safety stock demand that covers unplanned changes in demand

For modelling total safety stock this formula, modified from the approach Donald Waters (Waters 2003) describes two approximate safety stock requirements (see Fig. 2.4).

For the first part of the formula – safety stock supply – you need two input variables: average demand and supplier uncertainty. Average demand can be simply calculated by summing up demands from a number of time periods and dividing the sum by the number of time periods. Supplier uncertainty arises from orders taking different lengths of time to arrive from suppliers. It thus describes how reliable your supplier is. Let's take an example where:

Average daily demand = 500
Supplier uncertainty = 2 days

The equation of part (a) of the safety stock formula would look like this:

$$500 \times 2 = 1,000$$

Safety stock = (a) + (b)

(a) = Safety stock supply
(b) = Safety stock demand

(a) Safety stock supply

= Average demand x supplier uncertainty (SU)

(b) Safety stock demand

= Standard deviation of demand x service level factor x $\sqrt{LT + SU}$

Fig. 2.4 Modelling safety stock – approximation

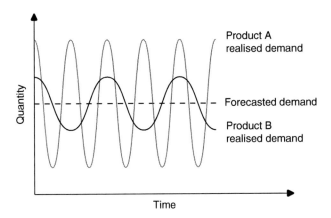

Fig. 2.5 Modelling safety stock – standard deviation of demand

Thus, in this example the safety stock held to protect for uncertainty in supply would be 1,000 units.

The second part of the formula is slightly more complicated. Let's therefore have a closer look at the safety stock held for demand uncertainty in more detail. The mathematical definition of standard deviation of demand is more difficult to understand than the concept. If you have a look at the next graph (see Fig. 2.5), which product has the greater standard deviation of demand?

By looking at the graph, we can clearly identify product A as the one with the greatest standard deviation of demand if we measure the distances of peaks and troughs of the line in comparison to the dotted forecasted demand line. The standard deviation of demand (or forecast error) can be defined as the deviation of the actual realised demand quantity from the forecasted quantity (see also Sect. 2.2.3 on demand planning improvements).

Next, we need to define the service level factor. For mathematical reasons, we cannot just insert our agreed 95% of service level into the safety stock formula. Instead we need to convert the 95% to a corresponding real number. In most inventory systems, it is assumed that items follow a demand distribution called the *normal distribution*. Statisticians have documented this in mathematical tables so that service levels can be equated to a number of standard deviations in order to derive the equivalent service level factor. A part of the conversion from service level percentage into service level factor can be seen in the next table (see Fig. 2.6).

Thus, if we have agreed a 95% service level with our customer the corresponding service level factor would equal 1.64. An example will now show how the safety stock demand can be calculated. Let's assume that:

Forecast error $= 50$
Service level factor $= 1.64$
Lead-time $= 4$ days
Supplier uncertainty $= 2$ days

The equation for part (b) of the formula would look like this:

$$50 \times 1.64 \times \sqrt{2+4} = 200.85 \approx 201 \tag{2.2}$$

Thus, in this example the safety stock held to protect for uncertainty in demand would be 201 units of inventory.

Service level in %	Service level factor (Standard deviation using the normal distribution curve)
50.0	0.00
70.0	0.52
75.0	0.67
80.0	0.84
85.0	1.04
90.0	1.28
95.0	1.64
96.0	1.75
97.0	1.88
98.0	2.05
99.0	2.33
99.5	2.57
99.8	2.88
99.9	3.09

Fig. 2.6 Modelling safety stock – service level factor

In order to get the total safety stock, we need to add up part (a) = 1,000 units and part (b) = 201 units. The final result of the approximate safety stock calculation would be 1,201 units.

There are more complex and sophisticated formulas used in safety stock calculation. For an extended discussion of this topic, the book "Inventory Control and Management" by Waters (2003) gives an excellent overview.

2.1.4 Reducing Inventory

There are several methods to reduce inventory. You can reduce cycle stock by ordering more often, such as every week instead of once a month. However there are four ways in which you can positively influence your safety stock position:

1. Reduce lead-time
2. Reduce supplier uncertainty
3. Reduce forecast error
4. Reduce service level

By compressing *supplier lead-times*, e.g. reducing it from four days to one day, less safety stock is needed to safeguard supply. The same applies for the reduction of *supplier uncertainty*. As suppliers become more reliable (ideally reducing their lead-time variability to zero), a considerably lower safety stock can be held. By *reducing forecast error*, demand uncertainty can be reduced and thus less safety stock will be needed. Lastly, the *reduction of service levels* will positively impact your safety stock position. This decision of reducing service levels to improve the overall safety stock position should be discussed and agreed together with your customer.

2.2 Demand and Supply Planning

2.2.1 Describing Demand

Demand can be segregated into various categories. These categories will help you to better understand demand. We will explore the following range of characteristics:

- Level of demand
- Frequency of demand
- Patterns of demand
- Product life cycle positioning
- Product classification

Let's start with the first one: *level of demand*. Demand for a certain item can be classified as high or low. The demand level of that individual item is always measured in relative terms to your total inventory. Thus, if you run a food retailing business in Asia, an item of high demand will be rice. Rice is an item of high demand because most families in Asia purchase and eat rice on a daily basis. A bottle of sparkling wine or champagne, on the contrary, may be an item of low demand in a food retailer's portfolio as champagne sells on a relatively lower level compared with other food items.

A further method of classification looks at the *frequency of demand* over a certain period of time. There are two main patterns: fast demand and slow demand (see Fig. 2.7).

The demand of items A, B and C as shown in the table occur on a regular basis each week. If you were to display this demand pattern graphically, you would find an even spread of demands around the average. This is known as a normal distribution and is generally accepted in most inventory systems as the expected pattern for all *fast-moving* items.

Slow items, on the other hand, display a less frequent demand pattern and have a number of periods with zero demand as indicated for items D, E and F. An example for a slow moving item in a car body shop would be a special carburettor whereas tyres would be classified as fast-moving items.

The third category of characteristics depicts the *patterns of demand*. Here, demand can be described as stable, trend or seasonal (see Fig. 2.8).

Stable demand can be described as demand that varies around a constant average over time. Thus, there are some fluctuations of demand in the various time pockets, but the fluctuations are small and we can fit a flat line through the various demand points. A *trend* demand pattern, in contrast, can be described as a demand pattern where the average demand can be described as an upward or downward sloping line. Thus, demand increases or decreases over time. The third form of demand pattern shows a pattern of *seasonality* throughout the planning cycle, e.g. 1 year. Market forces such as Christmas and Easter sales or external factors like weather can be the major influence for a seasonal demand pattern.

Product life cycle positioning is another category to describe demand. There are five distinct phases in a product life cycle (see Fig. 2.9).

In each of these phases, demand can take a different form and therefore could have an effect on planning and inventory management.

The *launch* phase often requires building up stock prior to the launch date. At this moment in time the demand level is at its most uncertain. Take for example the launch of the Nintendo Wii. Before its introduction, the rate of demand was very difficult to estimate. Soon after its introduction, it was clear that the demand resulting from this very successful launch could not be completely satisfied. It took the manufacturer some time to stabilise the supply in response to the accelerated rate of demand at product launch.

The next phase, the *emerging* phase, describes the demand building on the launch of the product. Depending on the growth rate of demand, the methods and techniques required to maintain the momentum of the launch will be chosen.

Once the product has moved to the *established* phase of the product life cycle, demand increases and decreases are still likely to occur but they will be less sudden and heavy in magnitude.

	Wk 1	Wk 2	Wk 3	Wk 4	Wk 5	Wk 6	Wk 7	
Item A	1	3	2	2	1	0	1	Fast
Item B	8	11	7	9	12	6	8	Fast
Item C	161	194	175	168	187	171	177	Fast
Item D	0	0	0	1	0	0	2	Slow
Item E	6	0	0	0	2	0	0	Slow
Item F	85	0	0	0	0	42	0	Slow

Fig. 2.7 Frequency of demand

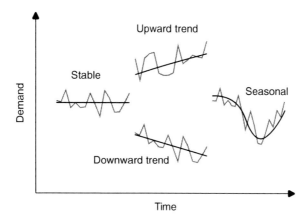

Fig. 2.8 Different patterns of demand

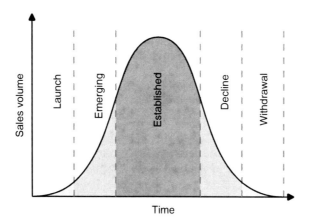

Fig. 2.9 Product life cycle

At some stage the product will enter the *decline* phase. Now the angle of decline of demand needs close monitoring in order to ensure that inventory levels are sufficient in order to meet ongoing demand.

When the product reaches the *withdrawal* phase demand is likely to approach zero and the product needs a good phase-out strategy in inventory control to minimise the risk of obsolescence.

The last classification category looks at product *segmentation* through the 80/20-rule (see also Chap. 4 on Make). Rather than spending the same amount of time for planning and managing every single Stock Keeping Unit (SKU), it is wise to segment the product portfolio into various product categories depending on their percentage turnover. Therefore, Pareto's law provides an approach to identify those items that will make the largest impact on your company's overall sales performance (see Fig. 2.10).

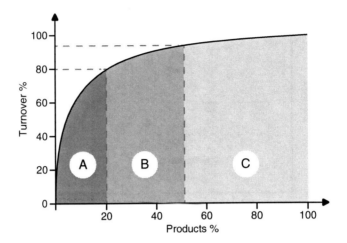

Fig. 2.10 Product segmentation using Pareto's law

This analysis is grounded in Pareto's law according to which 20% of the total number of items can represent as much as 80% of the total turnover.

A items	20% of items represent 80% of turnover	Fast movers
B items	30% of items represent 15% of turnover	Medium movers
C items	50% of items represent 5% of turnover	Slow movers

Therefore, we suggest that the first 20% of products are classified as "A items" or *fast movers* and receive special attention when it comes to statistical forecasting and inventory control. "B items" or *medium movers*, would form the next product group comprising roughly 30% of the items but representing only 15% of turnover. The last category of "C items" or *slow movers*, would consist of the last 50% of items and represents only 5% of the total sales value. These "C items" are sometimes called the tail of a product portfolio. Please note that companies might decide to include slow-moving and inexpensive items in the "A category" if these items are strategically important to the business or critical to one of the company's strategic customers even if their absolute sales value is low.

This classification is meaningful to planners and their managers as it helps focus attention on what is really important. This tool helps you to concentrate on the few vital "A items" and spend less time on the many trivial "C items". Where a classification solely based on percentage turnover is not appropriate, a multi-criteria approach can be pursued to base the classification of items on other criteria, such as lead-time, risk of obsolescence, product availability, substitutability and criticality.

2.2.2 Forecasting Methods

The last section showed how we could describe and classify demand. For production and inventory control reasons we now need some means of reducing uncertainty of the future. In part, this can be done by some estimate, prediction or forecast of future demand. The process of forecasting can therefore be described as the mechanism of arriving at measures for planning the future.

Many different approaches exist for forecasting future demand. When we speak about demand we mean the true demand of a single item. The lowest common denominator by which we distinguish one stock item from another is called the item-level SKU. Effective planning of inventory stock levels should be done through forecasts of each item level SKU.

There are two distinct classes of forecasting methods:

1. Qualitative forecasting
2. Quantitative or statistical forecasting

Qualitative forecasting includes the simple process of guessing future demand, making hunches based on intuition and using your experience. This includes judgment and common sense reasoning when establishing future demand. Whilst this set of qualitative techniques is often labelled as "unscientific" and bad business practice, most companies have realised the importance and value of using human reasoning and judgment in the inventory planning and forecasting process. For example, vuvuzela (the loud plastic horn) sales went up considerably in South Africa in the winter months of 2010. There are normally sales of these products for the football league supporters during this time. But there was another major event boosting vuvuzela sales that winter: the hosting of the football world cup. A forecasting system might not have forecasted this increased demand as there was no evidence for it in the past. An experienced planner, however, have used knowledge, judgment and a more holistic view of events to ensure adequate volume forecasts of vuvuzela sales.

Quantitative forecasting, on the other hand, comprises statistical models that can have a causal nature (for example, more ice cream sales with hot weather) or that can be based on time series of historical date. In fact, the time series method is the most common form of statistical forecasting. We will therefore explain this method in more detail in the next section.

2.2.2.1 Time Series Method

The time series method is a statistical forecasting method based on the assumption that historical patterns of demand are a good indicator for future demand. This assumption is also called the *assumption of continuity*. An example showing duty free purchases from the 1980s will illustrate the method (see Fig. 2.11).

In this example you can see past duty free purchases between 1981 and 1988 indicated in Fig. 2.11. The curve to the left of the dotted vertical line thus describes the past. After 1988 you can see an extrapolation of past data as the continued line into the future. This curve to the right of the dotted vertical line takes into account different aspect of the historic data and projects these 5 years into the future up to 1993. If we were to decompose the past duty free purchases, we could come up with at least three aspects: basic value, trend and seasonality pattern (see Fig. 2.12).

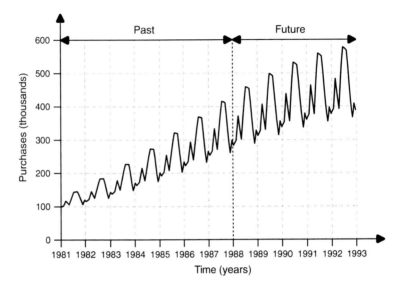

Fig. 2.11 Duty free purchases forecast

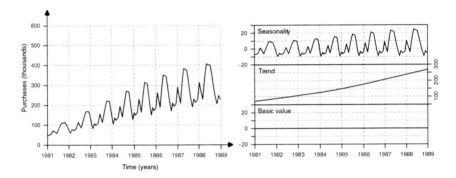

Fig. 2.12 Decomposition of demand

The basic value, also called the baseline in statistical forecasting, indicates the standard rate of sales that has been realised in the past. In this example, the baseline past sales amounted to 100,000 duty free purchases per year. Next, we can see a trend line that indicates an upward sloping trend. Thus, duty free purchases have increased over time at a certain rate. Lastly, we can observe a seasonal pattern throughout the years where sales peak around Easter and in the summer when people travel more and therefore sales increase.

Using the time series method, those three components are taken from the past and projected into the future using the assumption of continuity. This method is extremely powerful if a large amount of historical data exists and demand has not been massively affected by sales promotions or price reductions.

2.2.3 Demand Planning Improvements

There are a number of key performance indicators (KPI) that are important within the demand planning function. The following overview shows the act of balancing service, cost and demand planning improvements (see Fig. 2.13).

On the service side, demand planners need to make sure that their customer service KPIs in terms of case fill and order fill are met at all times. For more details on these two KPIs see Chap. 10 on Customer Service. Ideally, they hold adequate safety stock for each item to meet this customer service objective. Whilst customer service is at the core of most businesses, cost needs to be managed as well. Excess inventory can result in high costs associated with holding this extra stock and will increase the risk of obsolescence. As a consequence, stock that cannot be sold will have to be written off. In order to balance the cost-service trade-off, demand planning aims at improving forecast accuracy and reducing forecast error.

Forecast accuracy in the supply chain is typically measured using the Mean Absolute Percent Error (MAPE). Forecast error can be defined as the deviation of the actual realised demand quantity from the forecasted quantity:

$$Error(\%) = \frac{|(Actual - Forecast)|}{Actual} \tag{2.3}$$

This formula takes absolute values of the error because the magnitude of the error is more important than the direction of the error. Decreasing forecast errors will mean increasing forecast accuracy since forecast accuracy is the converse of error. Forecast Accuracy (FA) can therefore be defined as:

$$FA(\%) = (1 - Error(\%)) \tag{2.4}$$

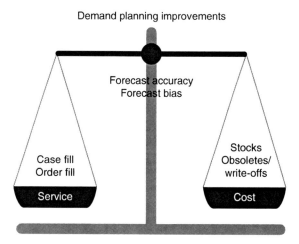

Fig. 2.13 Demand planning improvement measures

Let's have a look at an example calculation of forecast error and accuracy (see Fig. 2.14).

In this example you see a shop's doughnut sales forecasts and actual sales for 11 weeks. Using the formula as stated above, you find both forecast error as well as forecast accuracy for the various weeks in the last two columns.

2.2.4 Two Models of Order Cycle Management

After having discussed demand planning and forecasting aspects, let's now turn towards supply planning. The American sportswear and footwear retailer Foot Locker Inc., for example, buys shoes and apparel from international manufacturers such as Nike. For Foot Locker to manage inventory in their warehouses and distribution centres effectively, they need to decide when and how much to order. Let's start with the timing of the order first. According to Emmet and Granville (2007), there are two basic types of order policies: continuous review and period review.

In a continuous review system with a fixed order quantity, inventory is reviewed daily and a fixed quantity is ordered whenever the stock drops below a certain point. This point is called the *re-order point* (see Fig. 2.15).

An everyday example for continuous review and fixed order quantity would be a car driver filling up his fuel tank. When the driver sees the red light flashing he knows that he has hit the "re-order level". The driver tries to get to the nearest fuel station to re-fill the tank before it is empty. Many drivers always refill the same amount, such as €20. This steady top-up quantity can be seen as the fixed order quantity.

In a periodic review system with an order-up-to-level, inventory is reviewed at regular intervals and every time a sufficient quantity is ordered to raise the inventory level up to a certain level. This order quantity depends on the relative stock position at each moment of review, i.e. at each *review point* (see Fig. 2.16).

This model is also called *min-max policy* because the stock planner tries to keep inventory between a minimum and a maximum stock level. A family that goes grocery shopping on a weekly basis (e.g. every Saturday) is a good example for the periodic review model. A shopping list is created on Saturday morning by checking the levels of bread, milk and butter in the fridge and kitchen cupboard. The family knows how much it needs for 1 week (maximum stock level) and therefore writes down the required items on their shopping list: three loaves of bread, five litres of milk and two packs of butter.

Whilst with periodic review you can plan your stock purchases in advance, overall inventory levels will be higher. The family's kitchen cupboard and fridge will be full on Saturday evening after their weekly shopping trip in comparison to a typical student's review method, who is more likely to use the continuous review model. A student tends to keep very little in his fridge (the authors refer to their own experience here!) because of lack of cash. When they are hungry (reorder level) they go out and buy some food. Thus, the continuous review results in lower inventory levels, but possibly more frequent ordering.

Week number	Doughnut sales forecast	Doughnut sales actual	Forecast error	Forecast accuracy
1	80	100	20%	80%
2	80	110	27%	73%
3	100	120	17%	83%
4	100	130	23%	77%
5	150	140	7%	93%
6	150	150	0%	100%
7	200	160	25%	75%
8	200	170	18%	82%
9	175	180	3%	97%
10	175	190	8%	92%
11	220	100	10%	90%

Fig. 2.14 Doughnut forecast error and accuracy

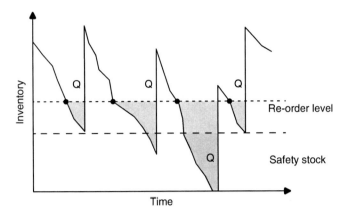

Fig. 2.15 Continuous review – fixed order quantity

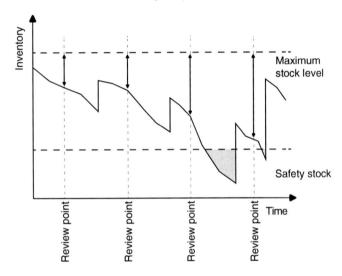

Fig. 2.16 Periodic review – fixed order cycle

In business, most slow moving "C items" from the 80/20-rule segmentation will be reviewed periodically. As a result, stock levels will be higher, but the order frequency will be lower. "A items", on the other hand, will be reviewed continuously as they are more important for the business and might move quicker.

2.2.5 The Economic Order Quantity (EOQ)

As an inventory manager you also have to ask yourself: How much should I order at a time? The trade-off lies in the cost of holding inventory and the cost of ordering it. If you decide to buy a large amount at once, the unit price may be low but you may have a lot more capital tied up in stock and it may require a large storage space. Furthermore, you may run the risk of obsolescence, especially in perishable items. If you order more frequently and smaller amounts, much less capital is tied up in stock, but the cost of raising a large number of orders may be higher.

One of the most commonly recognised models to solve this dilemma of inventory planning has been the concept of economic order quantity or EOQ first introduced by F. W. Harris. It is a method for calculating order quantities at individual SKU level (Norek 1998):

$$EOQ = \sqrt{\frac{2CR}{PF}} \qquad (2.5)$$

Where:
C = ordering cost per order
R = annual demand in units
P = purchase cost of one unit
F = annual holding cost as a fraction of unit cost
PF = holding cost per unit per year

Let's have a look at an example:

C = €20 average order cost
R = 3,000 annual demand
P = €12 unit cost of item
F = 0.25 (25%) average holding cost

For this example, the EOQ would give –

$$EOQ = \sqrt{\frac{(2 \times 3,000 \times 20)}{(12 \times 0.25)}} = \sqrt{\frac{120,000}{3}} = 200$$

Thus, in this example the economic order quantity would be 200 units. The optimum order quantity can be graphically represented at the point where the lowest total costs, consisting of ordering cost and inventory carrying costs, can be achieved (see Fig. 2.17).

This EOQ model, however, rests on a number of assumptions, some of which may be unrealistic for many product groups:

- The demand rate is known, constant and continuous.
- The supplier lead-time is known and constant.
- There are no stock outs permitted – since demand and lead-time are known stock outs can be avoided.
- The cost structure is fixed – order costs are the same regardless of lot size, holding cost is a linear function based on average inventory and unit purchase cost is constant (no discounts based on bulk purchase).
- There is sufficient space, capacity and capital to procure the desired quantity.

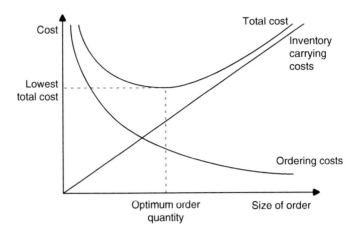

Fig. 2.17 The economic order quantity

It is obvious that these assumptions could make a very complex situation very simplistic.

2.3 Sales and Operations Planning

The term Sales & Operations Planning (S&OP) can be understood as a concept of integrated business planning. More specifically, S&OP can be defined as the process of constantly realigning decisions in sales, marketing, demand and supply planning areas with the aim to synchronise with the strategic financial plans.

2.3.1 The S&OP Process

The S&OP process is a multi-step process centred on a series of meetings (see Fig. 2.18).

The process starts with a series of pre-S&OP meetings. In the *demand planning* meeting, marketing, sales and demand planning teams gather all statistical forecasts, customer promotional plans and volume effects of marketing campaigns to show the most realistic future sales plans based on unconstrained demand.

The unconstrained sales plan is then passed on to the *supply and resource planning* team. In a pre-S&OP meeting, this team analyses the unconstrained demand plans against production plans, inventory availability and capacity constraints. At this point, the so-called "what-if" analysis are conducted to show several scenarios on how to minimise demand shortfalls in case of capacity constraints. The outcome of this meeting includes an operations and resource plan.

Next, the *finance integration* meeting takes place. In this meeting, the operations plan is reconciled with financial business goals. The output of the previous two

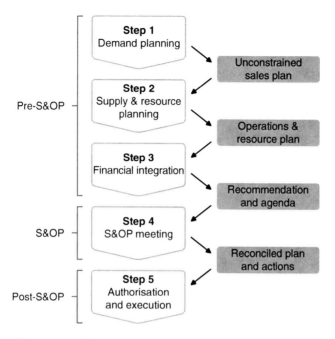

Fig. 2.18 S&OP process meeting structure

meetings is analysed against financial goals, based on revenue and profitability targets, business goals and customer service level commitments. The finance team builds on the "what-if" analysis and identifies demand-shaping opportunities that maximise the profitability where capacity constraints to customer demand exist. The financial team will come up with some recommendations as well as an agenda for the S&OP meeting.

During the actual *S&OP meeting*, which usually takes place on a monthly basis, all functional teams come together to discuss the reconciled demand and supply plans. This can be done using a stoplight system (green = okay, yellow = warning, red = problem) where all products or product groups are reviewed to identify the opportunities, risks and areas that need most attention according to the recommendations set by the finance team. This way, gaps can be identified, and gap-closing activities can be agreed. Once the plans have been agreed, the marketing organisation commits to making sure that the pricing and promotion programmes consistently support the plan.

The very important post-S&OP step is mainly about *authorising, executing and monitoring* the agreed plan. The tasks for the various teams include communicating the consensus plan to all teams as a blueprint until the next S&OP meeting cycle. Monitoring the operational progress against the plan is important at this stage of the process. KPI's such as forecast accuracy, profitability and revenue variances and customer service levels are utilised.

To summarise, S&OP is a set of business meetings and processes that enable the company to respond effectively to demand and supply variability. The outcome of the S&OP process is a reconciled plan that maximises financial and strategic opportunities and overall business profitability. The process aims to take place at regular intervals, e.g. on a monthly basis and typically looks at a mid to long-term planning horizon of four weeks to two years on a rolling forward basis.

2.3.2 Guiding Principles for Successful S&OP Implementations

According to Neil Lewis from Capgemini Consulting (Lewis and MacLean 2009), there are at least six principles that are crucial for any successful S&OP implementation:

1. *Stakeholder commitment* – It is important that stakeholders across the business are engaged and educated to understand the whole process. Therefore, clarification needs to be sought at an early stage as to who attends the input meetings, who makes the gap closing decisions and what supporting technology is being used. In addition, individual teams must be recognised and rewarded for walking that additional mile for the greater good of the business. Through these measures, stakeholders will feel committed and the overall S&OP implementation is more likely to be successful.

2. *One set of numbers* – In many businesses, more than one plan exists. Marketing might have a top down plan derived from the financial annual plan and spiced with expected uptake on new product innovations. Sales are likely to handle another set of numbers where promotional data and trade terms play a major role. The planning department is most likely to work with a volume forecast based on historical data. The aim of an S&OP initiative is to align these different plans and to form one set of numbers. All parties will now understand the deviations and risks and can jointly and proactively manage the plan.

3. *Accountability and decision making* – As the size of an organisation increases, so does the complexity in decision making. A multinational company implementing the S&OP process might have local, regional and global teams involved in the demand and supply process. This frequently makes it difficult to identify the true decision makers. In order to implement S&OP successfully, it is crucial to define in detail during the design phase what will be the participants role and responsibility in each meeting.

4. *Alignment of business objectives*– If one country's general manager's KPIs are linked to profitability and volume, the manager will try to deliver against these objectives, regardless of the impact on other parts of the business. The same applies to a production director, whose annual targets might be expressed as cost per case or operational efficiency, leading to longer production runs and higher levels of inventory. As long as these key stakeholders have different objectives and motivations, a common business process will be difficult to implement. Therefore, effective S&OP solutions have to align to KPIs that drive the best results for a company as a whole.

5. *Appropriate time horizon* – When things go wrong, the temptation is to micro-manage the crisis rather than to plan for the future. In order to function effectively, managers need to be freed from short-term thinking. In S&OP, the aim should be to maintain a medium to long-term focus. Moving the conversation into the future will help managers to reach best for business solutions, and therefore do less fire fighting on a daily basis.
6. *Understanding the benefits of S&OP* – Lastly, it is important to create a clear understanding of the S&OP benefits. A sound S&OP process recognises imperfections on a regular basis and re-optimises plans across the supply chain. It can optimise the network of factories and suppliers and will save in terms of stock holding. Most importantly, customers should benefit from better customer service and a more efficient response.

2.3.3 Customer Service Improvements Through S&OP

S&OP aims at improving your business, but how does S&OP make a difference in terms of customer service? The model below shows a three-step approach to customer service improvements through S&OP (see Fig. 2.19).

Through these three steps in the S&OP process, a business can achieve two intermediary outcomes: improved forecast and reconciled demand and supply. Both these outcomes will drive customer service improvement. But let's have a look at this step by step.

Step 1. From S&OP principles to improved forecast

There are three important characteristics in the S&OP process that will increase the demand forecast quality. First, there needs to be *consistency in the numbers*, i.e. the forecast is transparent and accessible for all functions involved. This forecast base should be stated in terms of *volume* (as opposed to value) because volume is really the "currency" driving the supply chain. Thirdly, all teams involved will agree the *consensus forecast*.

Step 2. From improved forecast to improved reconciliation of demand and supply

As a result of the steps taken to improve the forecast, the *forecast bias* will be reduced. Thus the actual sales will deviate less from the forecasted volume. Moreover, the forecast is tagged with *forecast drivers*, i.e. assumptions that underline the modelled peaks and troughs in the forecast. Finally, the forecast will reflect the mid to *long-term view* (rather then just the next two weeks) which gives the factories time to make those plans. Thus, the reduced forecast bias, the visibility of forecast drivers and the long-term view of the plan improve the quality of the reconciled demand and supply plan.

Step 3. From improved reconciliation of demand and supply to improved customer service

As an outcome of the improved reconciliation of demand and supply, the *supply plan* will be as realistic as possible at that point in time. Where supply doesn't meet demand, alternatives might be sought. If that is not possible, the customer will be warned at an early stage of a possible shortage. Based on that shortage information,

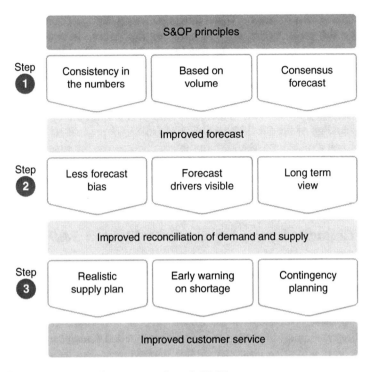

Fig. 2.19 Customer service improvement through S&OP

alternatives can be agreed collaboratively through *contingency planning*. If there is excessive supply, this information will be passed on as well in terms of new opportunities that are available. Together, this can be used for gap filling and additional promotions.

Thus, S&OP does lead to improved customer service by improving the forecast and the reconciliation between demand and supply.

2.3.4 Why S&OP Implementations Fail

There are several reasons why S&OP implementations fail. These can be described around the four categories:

- People
- Process
- Strategy
- Performance

First and foremost, it is essential to obtain executive-level *people* sponsorship. S&OP implementations fail if there is no top-down support for the agreed plan. Next, cross-functional teams need to be created consisting of marketing, sales, planning and finance team members. Naturally, there will be some tension between the functions so it is important to address these openly within the process. This way, organisational silos can be avoided that would otherwise harm the S&OP process.

Although the formal meeting structure is extremely important, effective S&OP involves more than holding monthly meetings. The project is also about producing real-time supply and demand visibility and making sure that business intelligence can be added continuously. If the organisation insists on sticking radically to the formal *process*, the S&OP implementation is likely to fail.

S&OP implementations have historically focused on merely balancing supply and demand volumes. In today's business *strategy*, it is also important to compare all planning scenarios on their profitability and strategic customer impact. Working collaboratively with customers has become one of the main ingredients of the S&OP project. Neglecting to do so can have a negative impact on the implementation.

Lastly, if you don't measure, you cannot improve. This risk of failure deals with the inability of an organisation to show, share and adjust their *performance* measures and metrics. All people involved in the S&OP process need to share the same vision and need to be measured along the same line. This will foster an environment of continuous improvement and business growth.

2.3.5 Different Planning Horizons

All steps in the supply chain planning process are linked and interact on the different planning horizons (see Fig. 2.20).

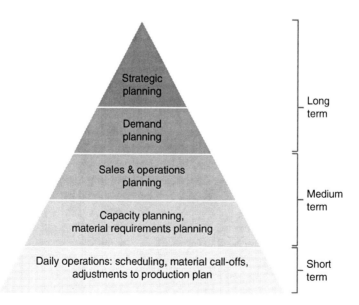

Fig. 2.20 Different planning horizons

Strategic planning, demand planning and sales and operations planning are considered long term planning activities. They interlink with the medium term capacity planning and materials requirement planning. The short-term activities centre on the daily operations in planning: scheduling, materials operational call offs and adjustments to production plans.

2.4   Case Study of Best Practice in Plan: Beiersdorf

Beiersdorf Italy reaches forecast excellence
Higher forecast accuracy and lower forecast bias achieved through improved sales forecasting processes
Beiersdorf is an international skin & beauty care company with leading global brands such as NIVEA, Eucerin and La Prairie. In 2007, demand planning project managers and local sales forecast managers elaborated the Integrated Sales Forecasting (ISF) concept as a company-wide best practice process. The underlying idea is cross-functional collaboration with respect to forecasting aspects especially for new products or promotional activities. Following these guidelines the Beiersdorf business unit in Italy has reengineered its forecasting process. The ISF process is the first step of implementing a complete S&OP process.
Before the implementation
Forecast accuracy (measured 13 weeks out) was at a level of about 45% wherefore the Italian business unit had to put special emphasis on its improvement. Because of these forecast accuracy figures and the high forecast bias, Beiersdorf struggled to get launch volumes right and to support their customers with sufficient promotional stock. As a consequence, sometimes fast moving personal care items suffered from OOS situations, whereas other slower moving items carried too much stock.
Company background
Traditionally, sales and marketing within Beiersdorf focused more on value than product mix specific volume forecasting. Due to frequent short-term changes in the product mix, Beiersdorf faced obsolete stock situations for certain products as well as excessive stock holding for others. In addition the capacity utilisation of the production centres should be increased. These facts led to a review of the supply network, which resulted in a reduced number of production centres and a change of the product allocation in the supply network. Accurate sales forecasting was thus even more important.
Another challenge that greatly impacted forecast performance was the "fear to remain without sufficient stock". This fear carried by some internal
(continued)

teams resulted in consistent over-forecasting, which consequently drove forecast bias up. The results were additional obsolete stocks. Therefore, Beiersdorf Italy was looking for an improvement plan.

Sales forecasting improvement plan

The implementation of the ISF process, which includes a monthly meeting cycle between sales forecast management, marketing, sales and controlling, was done with commitment from senior management. Mutually defined targets, a corresponding scheduling of activities and the contribution of all related departments ensured that all necessary information was shared between the groups. The most important barrier was to sensitise sales and marketing to the necessity to plan promotional activities more than 3 months in advance. In order to emphasise the importance of reliable midterm forecasting, it was demonstrated how high forecast accuracy could have a strong impact on a good service level as well as a reasonable stock situation.

The permanent education of the Italian sales forecasters also played a vital role in the overall forecasting process realignment. Lecturers from the Lancaster University Management School conducted forecasting workshops at the Beiersdorf headquarters in Hamburg. Vital knowledge and skills on statistical forecasting in the SAP APO demand planning software were gained and afterwards applied.

Improvement results

As a consequence of these improvement actions, forecast accuracy is now stable at a level of above 60%. Also the forecast bias, which measures tendencies to consistently over or under forecast demands, has improved and now shows a year-to-date value of -3%.

Due to increased complexity from customer requirements, the Italian business unit will increase their engagement in order to enhance their forecasting process more and more with market intelligence information. Further it is planned to start detailed analysis on market-based sell out data in comparison with sell in figures. Also, more steps towards implementing a fully integrated S&OP process with the factories are planned.

The successful realignment of Italy's forecasting process is a perfect example on how improved forecast accuracy and bias and ultimately increased sales can be achieved through an improved and integrated forecasting process.

Michael Tramnitzke
Project Manager Demand & Operations Planning
Beiersdorf AG
Alberto Duca
Sales Forecast Manager
Beiersdorf Italy

2.5   Suggestions for Further Reading

Plössl, G. W. & Orlicky, J. (1994). *Orlicky's material requirements planning*. New York: McGraw-Hill Professional.
Wallace, T. F. & Stahl, B. (2004). *Sales & Operations Planning: The "how-to" handbook*. Cincinnati, OH: TF Wallace & Co.

References

Emmet, S., & Granville, D. (2007). *Excellence in inventory management: How to minimise costs and maximise service*. Liverpool: Liverpool Academic Press.
Lewis, N., & MacLean, J. (2009). S&OP in a global world. *Supply Chain Management Review, 13*(1), 8–9.
Norek, C. (1998). Inventory management – Keeping costs down while lifting customer satisfaction. In J. L. Gattorna (Ed.), *Strategic supply chain alignment: Best practice in supply chain management* (pp. 381–392). Aldershot: Gower Publishing.
Waters, D. (2003). Inventory control and management. Chichester: John Wiley & Sons.

Chapter 3
Guide to Source in Supply Chain Management

Abstract This chapter guides you through the source function within supply chain management and is split into three main sections. First, it gives a definition of source and the pre- and post-order steps in the purchasing process. Second, it considers strategic sourcing initiatives with an overview of category sourcing management and supplier relationship management. Third, it considers sourcing management tools with a focus on negotiation and cost management. This chapter concludes with a case study of best practice when moving from local to global sourcing within the retailing company Sainsbury's.

Having read this chapter you will be able to:

- Explain sourcing and the purchasing process steps
- Clarify strategic sourcing initiatives
- Explore key management tools used in sourcing

3.1 Introduction to Sourcing

In our personal lives we are constantly busy with sourcing. When doing grocery shopping, buying a new car or seeking childcare, we decide on what specification we want and we identify suppliers from whom to buy. We may have to negotiate and we certainly have to pay. Sometimes we get involved in catalogue or home deliveries and we have all experienced service at different levels. We analyse and measure our suppliers by our experiences when doing business with them. In some instances, we even form an opinion about suppliers through word-of-mouth from friends and family, or we are influenced by commercial advertisements and what we see in the media.

In the business world a similar activity takes place on a large business-to-business (B2B) scale. Sourcing is one of the components of the supply chain operations reference model, and it is the interface between suppliers and the buying company. At high level we can split sourcing into two main business activities. The first one is selecting new suppliers. This includes finding suppliers that provide products and/or services that best meet the required needs, analysing them and

C. Scott et al., *Guide to Supply Chain Management*,
DOI 10.1007/978-3-642-17676-0_3, © Springer-Verlag Berlin Heidelberg 2011

Fig. 3.1 Effective sourcing benefits

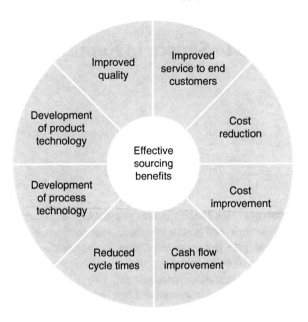

setting up contracts. The second main activity is then to manage the supplier over a period of time. This could be short, such as a one-off purchase such as a factory buying a new generator. Or it could be a much longer time period, such as a component supplier providing daily core materials for an electronics manufacturer over several years.

In terms of importance, sourcing is a key driver for bottom line improvement within organisations. If a sales force wins a €10 million contract and the contract gives a 10% margin, the contribution is a healthy €1 million for the business. However, if the sourcing team deliver €2 million savings, this is equivalent to a €20 million sales contract. One could argue that the sourcing team are performing better than the sales team! This bottom line contribution is enormously valuable yet often underrated in organisations.

There are many benefits organisations can achieve from managing sourcing well (see Fig. 3.1). Effective sourcing can, for example, lead to improved product quality or reduced order cycle times for customers.

Sourcing in product companies generally involves dividing products or services into two distinct groups: direct and indirect items (see Fig. 3.2 for some examples taken from a global drinks manufacturer). Direct items are directly related to the product's manufacturing process. Indirect items describe all other products and services that are needed to run the company.

Sourcing is a unique activity in the supply chain, as it is deployed in all organisations regardless of whether they have a supply chain or not. You do not need to be a manufacturing business to engage in sourcing. For example, the global bank HSBC will carry out a lot of sourcing activities.

Direct	Indirect
Glass	Factory security
Label	Consultants
Sugar	Cleaning products
Closure (cap)	Electricity
Flavouring	Protective clothing
Carbon dioxide	Stationery

Fig. 3.2 Examples of direct and indirect items

Different organisations refer to sourcing by different names. Although we might argue that the terms buying, purchasing, procurement or trading are all slightly different, they are used interchangeably in practice. Each organisation has different reasons for choosing one or the other term in their business language. For this chapter we shall use the term source.

This chapter provides the reader with an overview of the sourcing processes and tools. At the end, you will find recommendations for further reading to cover detailed subsets of sourcing.

3.1.1 The Purchasing Process: Pre-order Steps

The purchasing process is also known as the purchase-to-pay process (Monczka et al. 2008). The steps in the process may vary in different organisations, depending on the nature of the purchased item. New items may require more time upfront whereas repeat items usually already have approved sources. The purchasing process can be divided into two parts: the pre-order and post-order process. Let's have a look at the pre-order steps first (see Fig. 3.3).

To clarify each step in the pre-order process, let's consider how large fashion manufacturers organise their sourcing activities. Companies such as H&M (Sweden), Marks & Spencer (UK) or C&A (Germany) design fashion items in Europe but source large volumes of their products from manufacturing suppliers in Asia. For all of these global companies, it is important to have a robust purchasing process in place.

Firstly, the clothing company identifies the need for a product, for example a yellow dress with a unique design.

The design team finalises the *specification* for the dress, including material and accessories (e.g. clothing buttons/fasteners). They then work with their own buying team to make sure the buyers are clear on the specification for the clothing item. The buying team will also establish the commercial objectives at this step. This includes all their specifications from a potential supplier, for example cost, quality, service and lead-time for delivery.

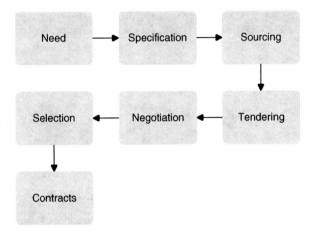

Fig. 3.3 Pre-order process

The buying team will then start looking for potential suppliers and thus start *sourcing*. The garment supplier might be a new trading partner or an existing one, depending on the specifications and capabilities.

Next, the buying team will select a short list of preferred suppliers. This is the start of the text process step called *tendering*. More details on the tendering process can be found in Chap. 11 on Outsourcing. The manufacturing suppliers will submit their tenders.

Negotiation will then follow with each chosen supplier where the detail of a potential buyer/supplier agreement is established. Items will be traded during this negotiation and the detail finalised.

From the supplier negotiations, the buying team will make their preferred supplier *selection*. The supplier that most appropriately satisfies the business needs outlined in the initial specification steps will be the ideal candidate.

The final pre-order step is the creation of one or several *contracts*. These will usually be prepared by the buying team, potentially using their legal team, and will clarify the detail supporting the buyer/supplier agreement. With both parties' signing the contract the pre-order steps are completed; therefore the yellow fashion dress is ready to be made and sold.

3.1.2   The Purchasing Process: Post-order Steps

With the contract in place between the clothing company and the supplier, this leads us to the post-order process (see Fig. 3.4).

The clothing company starts *placing their orders* on the manufacturing supplier for the yellow dress. In many B2B organisations the large volume of orders being placed mandate a process of effective *order handling*.

Fig. 3.4 Post-order process

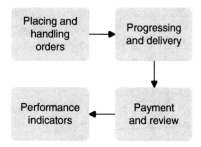

The clothing company then needs to monitor the *progress of the order* and *delivery*. This process step is split between two teams: the in-bound logistics team will be leading this step from the operational point of view, and the buying team is involved in case any service issues arise.

Once delivery is completed and the quantity reconciled with the order quantity, the clothing company will proceed with *payment and review* of the invoice, for each order in line with the agreed contractual terms.

The clothing company will review the supplier, usually at intervals specified in the contract. The review will generally be supported with a number of *performance indicators*, such as service and quality measures. The review has a two-fold objective. On the one hand, the review allows the buyer to address issues with the supplier. On the other hand, it gives the supplier – in this case the yellow dress manufacturer – a chance to give feedback on the feasibility of the contract.

3.1.3 Tactical Sourcing

The purchasing process of pre-order and post-order steps will continue on an operational basis daily. To help achieve the sourcing benefits described in the introduction an organisation can also carry out tactical sourcing. Tactical sourcing activities may be used in conjunction with the pre- and post-order steps or may sit outside. Some examples of tactical sourcing activities are:

- Market research
- Commodity analysis
- Forecasting requirements
- Supplier performance analysis and benchmarking
- Price and cost analysis

Continual *market research* is essential to establish what is happening in the market for a particular item or commodity. There may be a consolidation of suppliers due to mergers and takeovers that make suppliers more powerful.

There may be a shortage of a commodity item (e.g. the metal "copper") that could push up prices in the hi-tech sector or a bad harvest that would have a similar effect for food companies. Commodity items, both products and services, may represent a high percentage of a company's sourcing budget. *Commodity analysis* is therefore important for a business. As a result of the importance of commodity buying, organisations may recruit key individuals in their procurement functions, who have been sourcing the same commodities for a long time and are experts in the analysis of these items.

Supplier efficiency can be raised by communicating better *forecast requirements*. By improving supplier efficiency, reduced costs and improved service are juxtaposed for both parties. To achieve this, the sourcing team has to work on both the demand and supply side of the business. The team first establishes a robust forecast with the customers and then communicates the forecast to their suppliers.

The sourcing team should continually analyse supplier performance, costs, quality and service. This will include benchmarking against the suppliers' competitors, using the same criteria, to make sure the buying organisation is receiving the best output from its purchases. *Price and cost analysis* is a key part of this activity.

3.2   Strategic Sourcing Initiatives

We shall now consider some of the sourcing initiatives that are taking place in today's supply chain companies. As product companies have moved from a functional structure to a category management structure, category sourcing has become a strategic goal. The category sourcing concept also aims to achieve a shift in customer and supplier relationship, striving for joint benefits and co-ownership of the sale. This has moved organisations from short-term transactional relationships to more integrated relationships. A set of skills and way of working can be seen distinctly here in supplier relationship management.

3.2.1   Category Sourcing

Category Sourcing (CS) is a concept where the products an organisation requires are broken down into discrete groups of related products. A specific team is allocated for each product group or category. For example, in a large retailer a category might be "fresh food" and another "garden". These categories can be operated as stand-alone businesses within the organisation, often with their own profit and loss. The steps for a category sourcing process adapted from O'Brian (2009) are:

1. Profile the category group
2. Select the sourcing strategy
3. Generate the supplier portfolio
4. Follow the purchasing process
5. Negotiation

The first step is to *profile the category group*. In this step, the CS team will establish how many suppliers there are and what power they have. Power is an important concept in CS. The more powerful a supplier, the more leverage they have in negotiations. If a component can only be produced by one supplier and it is an essential part of a product, the supplier can dictate terms much more easily than if there were a hundred competing suppliers providing the same component.

The second step is to *select the sourcing strategy*. Using the correct CS strategy for a category is critical if the optimum sourcing benefits are to be realised. Buyers can choose what strategy to use; do they work closely with suppliers in face-to-face weekly meetings or do they communicate by telephone only on a monthly basis? Depending on how much the organisation spends and the risk to the business, if the chosen supplier fails to deliver, the sourcing team can use the appropriate strategy.

The third step is to *generate the supplier portfolio*. During this process step, potential suppliers that satisfy the required criteria, such as size, credit rating, company ethics, or sustainability requirements, are recorded.

The next step refers back to the pre- and post-order steps covered earlier in this chapter where the CS team *follows the purchasing process*.

The final step of *negotiation* is covered at the end of this chapter.

Going back to step one of the category sourcing process, the sourcing strategy matrix adapted from Kraljic (1983) is a tool to segment the different category groups (see Fig. 3.5).

We can see in the bottom left hand corner the *routine* items, which could be stationery in an organisation. These are low expenditure items and if the suppliers fail to deliver, there is usually little risk to the business.

Bottleneck items usually have a low spend but provide significant risk to an organisation if there is no supply. Bottleneck items are often low in number, but if out of stock, thus can stop production. A unique valve that is required in the oil production process is a good example for such a bottleneck item. If the valve breaks and there is no spare, the oil production halts.

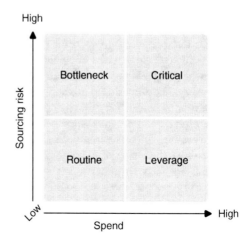

Fig. 3.5 The sourcing strategy matrix adapted from Kraljic (1983)

Leverage items are found in the bottom right corner. For a transport company, protective clothing is an example of a leverage item. The company spends a lot on protective clothing for the drivers, but there are many suppliers and it is not critical if a supplier fails to deliver. It is important to invest time in sourcing leverage items as there is an opportunity to reduce the money spent and make them routine items.

Finally, there are *critical* items in the top right corner. In car manufacturing, these could be the windscreens or car seats. These items, often bought in large quantities, can be classified as high in expenditure and high in risk. If no car seats and windscreens are supplied, car manufacturers like Audi and Renault can't deliver any cars to their customers.

The matrix is a useful way to categorise items and to set different strategies to manage risk. The matrix tells us that we should take different approaches when managing different categories. Whereas routine items can be simply bought online, critical items require more attention and some face-to-face interaction in managing the supplier relationship. For critical items, we would go through the entire purchasing process and have rigorous performance indicators with our suppliers in place.

3.2.2 Supplier Relationship Management

Supplier Relationship Management (SRM) is the process that looks at proactively managing the link between buyer and supplier. It is a mutually beneficial process that works in two ways and should improve the performance of both.

Some benefits of SRM include:

- Breaking down functional barriers and functional mindsets
- Promoting innovation and joint thinking for "doing things better"
- Improving supply chain visibility for buyer and supplier
- Sharing assets across supply chain, removing duplications
- Enhancing forward looking visibility giving more reliability to all parties

In SRM, there are different models of buyer and supplier interaction (see Fig. 3.6).

In the basic relationship approach – sometimes referred to as the bow-tie model – there is only one single point of contact (McDonald and Woodburn 2006). The basic relationship model is easy to manage as there are only two people involved in the B2B relationship. The downside of this approach is that decision-making might take longer, and the relationship is very much dependent on the two personalities in charge.

Therefore, an alternative approach is to create an interdependent relationship model (see Fig. 3.7). The interdependent approach looks very different and its set-up resembles the shape of a diamond. There are now many points of contact, and the main business customer teams work closely with the corresponding supplier teams. For example, the supplier's Research and Development (R&D) team work with the customer's marketing team. This way, the R&D team know what the customer wants to do in terms of marketing strategy and the customer's marketing team know the timescales and constraints of the supplier's R&D.

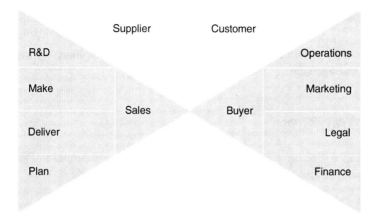

Fig. 3.6 Basic relationship approach
Source: McDonald, M. and D. Woodburn, Key account management: the definitive guide, Butterworth-Heinemann, Oxford, Copyright © 2006

Fig. 3.7 Interdependent relationship approach
Source: McDonald, M. and D. Woodburn, Key account management: the definitive guide, Butterworth-Heinemann, Oxford, Copyright © 2006

Unfortunately, a structure alone does not create sound SRM. There is a mindset change required and people within both suppliers and customers need to think differently. It is not enough for the customer to just have sourcing knowledge; they now need multi-dimensional business skills. Both buyer and supplier skills become less transactional and more consultative.

Finally, both parties need to develop a holistic relationship management approach, thinking about shared goals short-term individual gains. With the appropriate structure and armed with new skills, SRM can be adopted and benefits for both buyer and supplier achieved.

3.3   Sourcing Management Tools

We have selected two tools that are used very commonly in sourcing: negotiation and cost management.

3.3.1   Negotiation

The idea of a dispute or difference between two parties is central to the concept of negotiation: without disagreement between two parties there is no need for negotiating. Historically, mankind has developed a number of procedures for settling disputes, such as:

- By an act of violence
- Someone in authority decides – boss, judge, parent, teacher
- We take a vote
- By chance – draw lots or flip a coin
- By contest – competitive exam, race, test

If we use any of these procedures, we are not negotiating to reach an agreement. These gaps have been closed using different mechanisms but negotiation.

Central to the concept of negotiation is the process of giving and getting concessions. To make a concession means to give in. This does not necessarily mean that the seller lowers the price. There are other concessions that can be made, such as on the delivery terms or after sales service level.

In supply chain sourcing, negotiation usually takes place between two parties: the buyer and the supplier. It does not matter which side of the table we sit at, in negotiation we each follow the same negotiation process.

The four main stages of negotiation are:

1. Establish if negotiation is required
2. Plan the negotiation
3. Execute the negotiation
4. Deliver the agreement

Imagine an organisation buys one low cost item that has a set price; in this case negotiation is not required. Negotiation has a cost associated with it so that before investing time in the four-stage process we must first *establish if negotiation is required.*

If we decide that the four-stage process is required, then we need to *plan the negotiation.* Planning the negotiation well increases the chance of success. In the planning stage you should create your wish list – items that are of high value to you, but hopefully low cost to the other party. Here you must also agree on the separate roles that you will be representing, including the chief negotiator, summariser (who helps to buy thinking time and clarifies the agreement at each stage) and any observers you wish to appoint. Finally, the selection of the negotiation site is

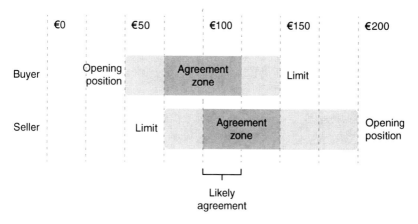

Fig. 3.8 Agreement zones for buyer and supplier

important: do you wish to conduct this on "home turf" or decide to choose a neutral venue?

The agreement zone is a very important part of the plan. It is the realistic outcome of where you can afford to be in a negotiation. An example is shown in Fig. 3.8.

We can see that the buyer has an agreement zone from €75 to €125. However the seller has an agreement zone between €100 and €150. If the buyer opens with a price of €50 against the seller at 200, then clearly there is a big difference. Concessions will need to be given by both parties if agreement is to be achieved along the overlap between the two agreement zones.

Executing the negotiation follows as the next step. After planning, the execution phase is most important in negotiations. To optimise this step, you may decide to:

- Set a public and joint agenda, to manage the scope and time for the negotiation.
- Focus on making proposals. Propose, don't argue and base statements on facts.
- Trade, using "If ... then" and don't give concessions away for nothing.
- Use and observe tactics from the other side.
- Close effectively and don't give away last minute concessions because you're pleased with how it went.

The final stage of the process is to close the deal and to *deliver the agreement*.

3.3.2 Cost Management

Let's now have a look at cost management, the second tool in sourcing. You can break down the total product cost into three elements:

- Fixed costs
- Variable costs
- Semi-variable costs

A supplier's fixed costs remain constant with different levels of volume and could be factory site rental or insurance. *Variable costs* change with volume and could be temporary labour at busy times. *Semi-variable costs* could be the supplier's management team, who have a base salary that is fixed, but a bonus that is variable when certain volume targets are hit.

In terms of managing these costs strategically, there are some sourcing tools that are commonly used:

• Commodity purchasing
• Value engineering and analysis
• Non-value added improvement
• Total cost of ownership
• Price analysis

Commodity purchasing can constitute a large proportion of an organisation's spend. The strategy for commodity purchasing should consider negotiation, volume leveraging and global sourcing.

Value engineering and analysis both involve working with suppliers to initiate any new product development processes more effectively, as well as to consider design and specification improvements.

Non-Value Added (NVA) improvements involve working with suppliers to remove waste. Eliminating production down times, excess inventory and long order cycle times are good examples for NVA optimisation.

The concept called Total Cost of Ownership (TCO) is important for buyers as it considers selecting the lowest cost of supply, not the lowest price. Let's imagine the purchase of a new refrigerator for our kitchen. We do a search on the Internet and find two suppliers that both sell the same brand and type but at different prices. Retailer A sells our fridge at €90 and retailer B at €110. Looking at prices only, the decision is clear: we buy from retailer A as he offers the lowest price. However, due to environmental legislation refrigerators have be returned and disposed in an environmental-friendly way (see Chap. 6 on Return). Whereas retailer B includes a end-of-life collection policy on disposal in the €110 offer, retailer A doesn't but would charge an extra €60 on top of the €90. If we assume a very low cost of capital for this ten-year period, the TCO for retailer A's refrigerator is €150 (€90 plus €60). Now retailer B offers the better deal with the lower TCO at €110. Keeping the total cost of ownership in mind, we would now probably opt for retailer B.

The last tool in cost management is *price analysis*. A price analysis model is shown in Fig. 3.9.

Let's consider the price of an item from a small supplier providing units of packaging for a large pharmaceutical company. The pharmaceutical company's sourcing team analyses the price and establishes the material cost at 60%, the value added contribution at 30% and the supplier profit at 10%. The value added contribution could be, for example, the supplier factory conversion cost and transportation to its customer.

Reducing the *profit* of the packaging supplier is a target for a buyer, but if excessive it could lead to the supplier going out of business.

Fig. 3.9 Price analysis
model

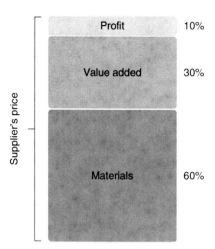

Value added cost could be reduced by the pharmaceutical company sharing best practice manufacturing processes with its smaller suppliers.

A contemporary sourcing approach would be to work with the supplier to jointly reduce the *material* costs. In this case, the pharmaceutical company already buys high volumes of materials so could buy materials on behalf of its smaller supplier using its purchasing power.

3.4 Case Study of Best Practice in Source: Negotiations

A different perspective on making the deal

Negotiating sourcing arrangements is not simply about securing the best deal – it is about securing the best deal and ensuring that the sales relationship continues into the future. A car salesperson, for example, wants to sell a car at the highest price, but also would like the customer to return year after year to buy cars from them in the future. Normally, each party has an existing relationship or indeed would like to build a future relationship. It is difficult for either party to quantify the value of the relationship.

Therefore, Ertel (1999) suggests that we categorise the issues in a negotiations situation into two elements:

1. Deal issues and
2. Relationship issues

(continued)

Deal issues refer to the terms and conditions of the service level agreement. They mainly concern unit price, lead-times and service parameters.

Relationship issues are softer and evolve around trust and respect of each party. Sourcing relationships build over time and can be destroyed easily if one party feels badly-treated or even betrayed.

By distinguishing the deal from the relationship, the negotiation can be handled more effectively. Ertel's concept furthermore recognises that each party needs to share information freely in order to build the relationship, whilst still maintaining independent goals and targets to get the best possible deal agreed. But how does this work in practice?

A model that is useful when applying negotiation and relationships has been developed by psychologists and learning specialists and has been extensively adopted in the field of Neuro-Linguistic Programming (NLP) (O'Connor 2001). NLP is an approach to organisational change, and it is based on a model of interpersonal communication. The model that O'Connor uses in the context of negotiations consists of six levels:

1. Environment – the where and when
2. Behaviour – the what
3. Capability – the how
4. Beliefs – the why
5. Identity – the who
6. Beyond identity – the connection

To make this model work, you need to make a connection to the other negotiation party at each of these six levels. You may choose to either make this connection by aligning and building rapport at each level, or you may choose to not align your connection – depending on your negotiation strategy. You can be trained to connect more or less at each of these levels, and to illustrate the concept, we will refer to examples from our experience as business trainers on some of these levels.

Building a connection at the *environment level* could be implemented by sharing the same dress code. In the training environment, we model the impact of dressing differently and recording the change it has in connecting to the other person.

At the *capabilities level*, a connection could be established through showing success in your business. In the training environment, we model the different outcomes when negotiating with an "internal supplier" compared to an "external supplier".

At the *beliefs level*, a connection exists when both parties in the negotiation have deep respect for and understanding of each other's values. Interestingly, they don't have to share the same values, but recognise and tolerate those of the other party. For example, if the buyer has a football team she

(continued)

supports and the seller also supports a football team, then the connection can be made without them both cheering for the same team.

To summarise, as we strive to mature our sourcing relationships to grow interdependent, we must keep the different NLP connections in mind in order to build trust – all the way through the negotiation cycle.

3.5 Suggestions for Further Reading

Baily, P., Farmer, D., Crocker, B., Jessop, D., Jones, D. (2008). *Procurement principles and management*. Harlow: Financial Times Prentice Hall.
Carter, R. J. (2006). *Practical procurement*. Cambridge: Cambridge Academic Press.
Fisher, R., Ury, W., Patton, B. (1991). *Getting to yes*. New York: Penguin Books.
Luecke, M. (2003). *Negotiation: Your mentor and guide to doing business effectively*. Harvard Business Essentials. Boston: Harvard Business School Press.

References

Ertel, D. (1999). Turning negotiation into a corporate capability. *Harvard Business Review, 77*, 55–71.
Kraljic, P. (1983). Purchasing must become supply management. *Harvard Business Review, 61*(5), 109–117.
McDonald, M., & Woodburn, D. (2006). *Key account management: The definitive guide*. Oxford: Butterworth-Heinemann.
Monczka, R. M., Handfield, R. B., Giunipero, L. C., & Patterson, J. L. (2008). *Purchasing and supply chain management*. Florence, KY: South-Western Publication.
O'Brian, J. (2009). *Category management in purchasing: a strategic approach to maximize business profitability*. London: Kogan Page.
O'Connor, J. (2001). *The NLP workbook: The practical guidebook to achieving the results you want*. London: Thorsons.

Chapter 4
Guide to Make in Supply Chain Management

Abstract This chapter guides you through the make function of supply chain management. It is important to understand this function as it describes the most capital-intensive step in many product supply chains. This chapter is split into three sections. First, the make function is introduced along with manufacturing planning and control as part of the manufacturing set up. Second, the concept of just-in-time and its impact on manufacturing efficiency is presented. Third, lean thinking and tools for improvement will be depicted. The chapter concludes with a case study of best practice on lean manufacturing within the company Unipart.

Having read this chapter you will be able to:

- Explain what the make function is and how it fits into the supply chain
- Clarify how to set-up manufacturing
- Identify just-in-time strategies and their value for manufacturing efficiency
- Recognise how lean thinking tools and techniques can improve the manufacturing process

4.1 Introduction to Make

Moving on to the next function in the SCOR model, the term make describes the process that transforms inputs into outputs, e.g. raw materials into finished goods. Make is also known as the manufacturing, assembling, processing or manufacturing function, and can be defined as the physical act of making the product. We shall use the term manufacturing in this guide. This includes the people who work in manufacturing (*man*), the business process to run manufacturing (*method*), the technology employed (*machine*) and the materials consumed (*material*).

4.1.1 From Craft to Mass Manufacturing

Manufacturing started with craft manufacturing where items such as shoes, horse carriages and pottery used to be made by hand and with the aid of tools. Craft

C. Scott et al., *Guide to Supply Chain Management*,
DOI 10.1007/978-3-642-17676-0_4, © Springer-Verlag Berlin Heidelberg 2011

manufacturing was the common method of manufacture for all common goods in the pre-industrialised world.

There are several advantages of craft manufacturing: the product is unique and of extremely high quality. However, this uniqueness can be disadvantageous as seen in the case of early automobiles, where every replacement part had to be manufactured from scratch (or at least customised) to fit a specific vehicle.

With the industrial revolution in the early twentieth century, mass manufacturing, popularised by Henry Ford's Motor Company, replaced craft manufacturing in many industries. In mass manufacturing, all parts were now standardised which guaranteed a replacement parts' compatibility with a variety of vehicle models. Other advantages of mass manufacturing (in comparison to craft manufacturing) were the reduced manufacturing time and therefore the greater manufacturing output. Human error and variation was also reduced as process steps were highly standardised and tasks were predominantly carried out by machinery.

Today, most common goods and consumer products are manufactured with the help of machinery and mass manufacturing. Industries that used to be craft manufactured, like fashion clothing, are now mainly mass-produced. Mass manufacturing today is mostly supply driven, i.e. products are produced before the customer demands them, as modern customers are not willing to wait for the manufacturing of a T-shirt or a salad bowl anymore, and prefer to buy them from stock.

The degree of customisation may differ in the manufacturing process of today. The car industry uses different manufacturing set-ups depending on the kind of car, i.e. a Toyota is produced in a different way than a Lamborghini. However, one thing is for sure: The process of making something by hand has been largely replaced by automation, computerisation or the use of manufacturing robots. Whilst *machine* has become more important in the make process, this does not mean that *man*, *method* and *material* have lost their ranks as will be shown in the next sections.

4.1.2   Five Types of Manufacturing Process

Businesses have a range of choices to make between different modes (*method*) of manufacturing depending on the nature of the product and the target market. There are five classic types of manufacturing process:

- Project
- Job shop
- Batch
- Line
- Continuous flow

Each of these will be explained in the following sections giving examples of industries that make use of each specific type of manufacturing process.

4.1.2.1 Project

The so-called project process is a one-off manufacturing process that meets very specific customer requirements and that is too large to be moved once completed, e.g. the Bird's Nest Olympic stadium in Beijing.

4.1.2.2 Job Shop

The job shop is also a one-off manufacturing process where the end product meets the unique order requirements of a customer. Job shop manufacturing is different from the project type as assembly usually takes place offsite. Once completed, the product, e.g. a luxurious yacht, is being delivered to the customer.

4.1.2.3 Batch

Batch manufacturing is also known as flow manufacturing, where similar items are provided on a repeat basis usually in larger volumes. In batch manufacturing, the process is divided into a chain of activities that take place after each other, e.g. Benetton runs batch processes on dying, cutting, sewing and packing their seasonal garments.

4.1.2.4 Line

In a line process, products are passed through the same sequence of operations from beginning to the end. Line manufacturing can be made to order, e.g. cars in an assembly line at BMW or they can be made to stock, e.g. fridges or washing machines at Siemens.

There are two common forms of cell arrangements used in the make process of line manufactured products: the U-line cell and the rabbit chase cell (see Fig. 4.1).

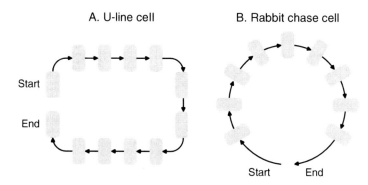

Fig. 4.1 Common cell arrangements in manufacturing

When the machines are placed in the shape of a narrow U, we speak of a U-line cell. A worker with sufficient skills can perform all the operations on a part by following the product along one side of the U, around the close end of the U and back up the other long side of the U. When there are two operators assigned to the U-line cell, then the machines will be split up between the two. Having two or more workers in the U can increase the rate of output.

In a rabbit chase cell, the machines are arranged in a circle, with the operator side of the machines facing the centre. By moving around in a small circle the operator can follow the product using all of the machines. The cycle time can be shortened if some of the machines are automated.

4.1.2.5 Continuous Flow

This type of manufacturing applies to certain products that run continuously through various refining, cooling and separating steps in the manufacturing process. In continuous flow manufacturing, the choice of process is based on the liquid or gas-like product nature and high volumes, which justifies the very high investment involved. Most petrochemical companies, such as Exxon and Shell, operate continuous process set-ups, as do providers of water and gas.

4.1.2.6 Other Set-Up Considerations

Product companies can implement a combination of these five types of manufacturing processes. Imagine a company, for example, that has low demand volumes of finished goods but may contain common components that are needed in high volume. This company may implement a line and job shop manufacturing at the same time. The volume of common components may be high enough to justifying a line process, whereas the assembly of the finished product is done in a job shop process.

Each choice of process will bring certain implications for the business in terms of response to its markets, manufacturing capabilities and level of investment required. Depending on the type of product, the business might not have a real choice in which manufacturing set-up to choose. A petrochemical company will, for example, not have another choice but to implement continuous processing for its oil-refining process. However, it is still of paramount importance to be aware of the business implications and the trade-offs in comparison to other process choices.

When moving from project or job shop manufacturing to batch, line or continuous flow, certain *machine, method, materials* and *man* features change as the overview shows. (see Fig. 4.2).

For example, the variety of different products made declines as the manufacturing set-up is shifted towards batch, line or continuous flow manufacturing. Likewise, the process becomes more rigid and standardised. As variation decreases and standardisation increases, control over the exact delivery time of finished goods to customers

From project manufacturing to continuous flow

Machine	Number of different kind of products made declines Product volume increases from, one-off to, mass market Product standardisation increases and customisation declines
Method	Process becomes more rigid and standardised Equipment is more specialised Operations become larger with economies of scale
Material	Control over delivery time of finished products become greater Work in progress inventory is minimised Finished goods inventory is larger than other inventories
Man	Manual labour content decreases relative to product value Job variety decreases Labour is hourly paid rather than by incentive

Fig. 4.2 Changes to manufacturing methods

becomes greater. As a consequence for the people working in the manufacturing process, their job variety decreases and they are more likely to be paid on an hourly basis than by the incentive to deliver the finished project or product.

4.1.3 Manufacturing Planning and Control

Once the manufacturing set-up is clear, we need to establish methods or systems in order to plan and control the transition from input, into output. Extensive literature is available on the topics of the Master Production Schedule (MPS) and Material Requirements Planning (MRP). A good book for further reading is Plössl's book on MRP (Plössl and Orlicky 1994). The manufacturing planning and control process can be depicted in a simple diagram (see Fig. 4.3).

In fact, manufacturing planning can be compared to preparing a dinner at home, and we will try to draw on this analogy whenever possible.

4.1.3.1 Master Production Scheduling

Let's start with the MPS. When preparing your dinner, you are quite likely to think about the following questions a few days earlier:

- What type of food will they want to eat?
- How many guests do I have?
- Are there any specific requirements for the guests?

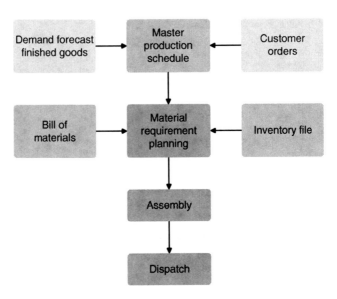

Fig. 4.3 Manufacturing planning process flow

Effectively you are constructing a type of master manufacturing schedule to define all the parameters. In manufacturing this is no different. A MPS is built up from *demand forecasts* that are established for end products and end customers (type of food and number of guests). The MPS can also be built with *customer orders* instead of demand forecasts if available. Going back to the dinner example, a customer calling a restaurant to order a vegetarian meal in advance could be classified as a confirmed order.

MPS is the first step in the implementation of the overall manufacturing programme of a factory. It has two main objectives. The first objective looks at the short-term *material requirements planning*. The second objective is about the long-term estimate of demands on company resources, i.e. man and machines.

It can be considered the output plan for the factory and is constructed by feeding actual demand forecasts and customer orders into the *master production schedule*.

In our dinner example we only prepare a one-off event, thus it is different from a manufacturing environment where the MPS usually continues over a longer horizon as factories produce continually. In reality the plan is often ongoing into a 3–36 months horizon that can contribute to the complexity of the schedule. To simplify the MPS, the factory planner does not normally plan every single product or SKU individually, but inputs plans according to product groups. Depending on the nature of the business, the planner has to select the appropriate level of aggregation in each case.

An example of a continuous schedule can be seen in the master schedule grid for product families X, Y and Z (see Fig. 4.4).

Plan version 1

Product	March	April	May	June	July	August	Sept
X	100	90	10	0	0	75	0
Y	120	80	60	120	40	20	0
Z	35	0	10	35	0	20	0

Plan version 2

Product	March	April	May	June	July	August	Sept
X		90	10	0	0	50	60
Y		80	60	120	40	20	0
Z		0	10	35	0	20	20

Plan version 3

Product	March	April	May	June	July	August	Sept
X						-25	60
Y							
Z						20	20

Fig. 4.4 Continuous schedule example

The factory planner first enters the plan in the plan version 1 and then updates the schedule as time progresses in plan version 2, once better demand information is available. The planner works on a 6 month rolling horizon so the output planned for September is added at the end of March. The last grid shows the net change between consecutive plans version 1 and 2. In this case the planner has reduced product X by 25 units in August, as new demand information has been made available.

The planner has changed August, month six, at the end of the planning horizon. It may have been much more difficult if the planner had changed April, month one, at the beginning of the MPS. If the quantity in month one is increased at short notice, it might be quite difficult for the business to source the right quantity of raw materials and components in time. Conversely, if month one is reduced at short notice, it is likely that the factory will be left with excess components and raw material. The business needs rules that dictate when the MPS can be changed.

An approach to manage this manufacturing planning challenge through different MPS horizon segments is shown (see Fig. 4.5).

The business in this case is planning 15 months ahead and so-called "time fences" separate the different planning horizons from another. For example, the first 6 months from April to September are fixed and cannot be changed. The next 3 months are flexible and can be changed up to 50% in increases or decreases. The final 6 months are totally flexible and can be changed as time gets closer to the demand and more accurate forecasting can be achieved.

4.1.3.2   Materials Requirements Planning

Let us return to our dinner analogy. With the preparation of the menu, the number of guests and the acknowledgement of special requirements, the MPS can be produced. We now know what type of food and how much is required for our guests.

You as the chef will now plan as a second step, the material requirements for the dinner by answering questions such as:

- When and at what time will the guests want to eat?
- Where and when do I need to collect the food ingredients?
- Will any of the products perish, so I need to pick them up on the day of the dinner?
- Are any of the ingredients long lead-time products so I need to order them well in advance?
- Which suppliers shall I use for each ingredient?
- What ingredients have I already got in the kitchen?

You are now moving from MPS into MRP. The aim of MRP is to ensure that items are available for manufacturing when they are needed: not after and not before. It works by synchronising ordering and delivery from suppliers with the factory's planned requirements. MRP has two main inputs:

1. Bill of materials
2. Inventory file

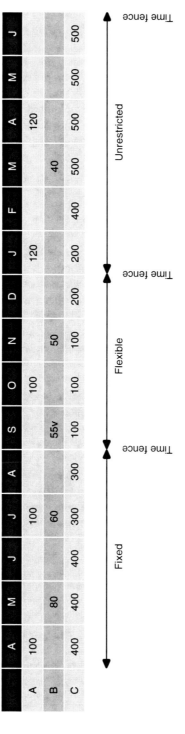

	A	M	J	J	A	S	O	N	D	J	F	M	A	M	J
A	100			100			100			120			120		
B		80		60		55v		50				40			
C	400	400	400	300	300	100	100	100	200	200	400	500	500	500	500

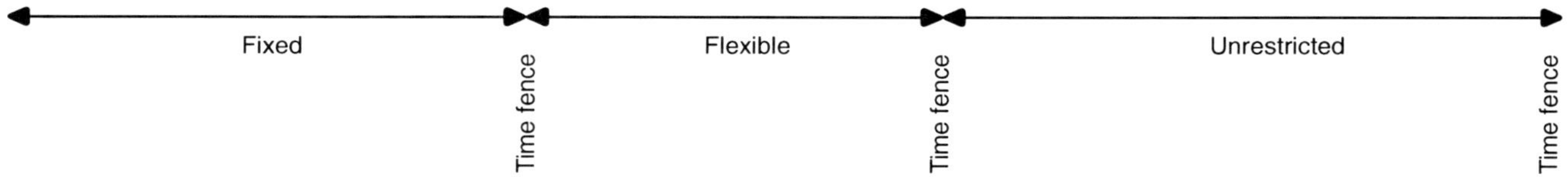
Fixed
Time fence
Flexible
Time fence
Unrestricted
Time fence

Fig. 4.5 Different MPS horizons

The product structure or *Bill of Materials* (BOM) is the "recipe" for a product. The BOM states what components are required for our dinner. Finally the *inventory file* will state how many of the required components are already in stock and therefore will not be purchased anymore. The *inventory file* states how much material is available (on hand). The *inventory file* is important, as the total requirements will be netted against the inventory on hand.

The MRP system will now have all the required inputs. It will allow the planner to have a clear plan of order quantity and timing for each component or raw material. These orders should then arrive available for *assembly* and not before. The manufacturing plan can now be executed, i.e. the cooking of the meal to come back to our dinner example.

4.1.3.3   Other Make Planning Concepts

There are two additional key planning concepts within manufacturing: Capacity Requirements Planning (CRP) and Distribution Requirements Planning (DRP).

CRP is the process of determining the impact on key resources required to support the proposed manufacturing plan. When carried out at a high and aggregate level it is called Rough Cut Capacity Planning (RCCP). Using the example of making dinner for your guests, you will need to confirm some time before the event that you actually have got enough oven space (*machines*) and kitchen help (*man*) to make the dinner. Likewise, manufacturing planners need to ensure that they have enough manufacturing capacity to produce what the business requires. If there is not enough capacity, a business may decide to outsource capacity or build more factories in the long term. With too much spare capacity and a low utilisation, however, a factory closure or moving capacity to other factories may be considered. This is often completed at an "above country/market" level.

A DRP system focuses on the planned delivery of finished products to customers and is in a way very similar to MRP. Instead of material requirements, customer orders, finished goods volumes and preferred delivery times are inputted into a DRP system. The system will then calculate and support the coordination of finished product delivery or deployment to those customers.

4.2   JIT Manufacturing Strategies

We have now discussed how manufacturing can be set-up, planned and controlled. Next, we will discuss approaches and strategies of how to run this function efficiently.

The concept of Just-In-Time (JIT) offers an approach that organises all activities in the make process so that they happen exactly at the time that they are needed: not before and not after. You can see the effect when you order a taxi to go to the airport at 8:00 in the morning. If the taxi arrives at your house at 7:30 a.m., you are not ready yet and the taxi driver wastes time while waiting for you. If it arrives instead at 8:30 a.m. you are very unhappy because you are likely to miss your flight – probably you will not use the same taxi driver again. But when the taxi arrives at 8:00 a.m. – just-in-time for your trip – the taxi driver does not waste time and you are happy with the service.

Though JIT seems an obvious concept, it is worthwhile looking into its characteristics in more detail. If we compare conventional manufacturing companies to those progressive ones using the JIT concept, we can observe the following difference. Conventional companies experience long set-up times, transportation and lead-times. Inventory, floor space and lot sizes are likely to be large. In addition, defect rates and machine breakdowns will be high for the conventional firm as well. In comparison, the progressive company will have short set-up, transportation and lead-times. Inventory, floor space and lot size will be small and machine defects will be reduced for these organisations. Overall, the manufacturing processes run smoother and more efficient than with the conventional companies.

What is the difference? The difference is the use of JIT manufacturing that began as a method of reducing inventory levels and has now developed into a comprehensive management philosophy. We will have a look into the JIT philosophy and its concepts next.

4.2.1 JIT Philosophy

JIT is a management philosophy that has been practiced in Japanese manufacturing organisations since the early 1970s. JIT was first developed and tested by Taiichi Ohno within Toyota's manufacturing plants. Mr. Ohno and his team first developed the Kanban (Japanese for *signboard*) system, which involves the use of cards to indicate where manufacturing materials are needed. The Kanban philosophy states that parts and materials should be supplied at the very moment that they are required: not before and not after that. JIT extends Kanban while linking purchasing, manufacturing and logistics to each other. Faced with constraints in the end-to-end supply chain process, Mr. Ohno and his team worked towards achieving the optimal cost/quality relationship in the Toyota manufacturing process.

Let's have a look at the river of inventory that is often drawn in Japan to explain the philosophy behind JIT (see Fig. 4.6).

The level of the river represents inventory and the company operations are visualised as a boat that navigates up and down the river. When the level is lowered, rocks are exposed. These rocks symbolise problems such as poor quality, supplier delays and inaccurate forecasts.

In many developed economies, the way to deal with those rocks, i.e. problems, was to maintain or increase inventory and thus introduce more safety stocks. This covers up the problems. In the first picture A, the boat floats above the rocks and does not have to navigate around the rocks. No manufacturing problems seem to be present.

a Traditional approach

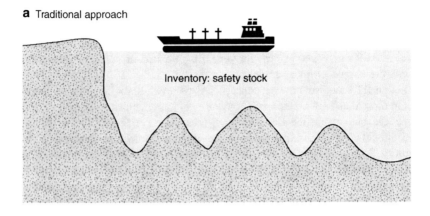

b Just-in-time approach

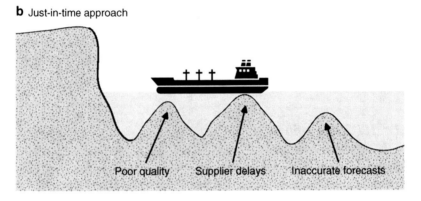

Fig. 4.6 The river of inventory

By contrast, Mr. Ohno and his colleagues at Toyota wanted to uncover the rocks. As a core element of their JIT philosophy, the Ohno team systematically reduced inventory by facing and resolving problems. Cutting safety stocks revealed inefficiencies in the manufacturing process that can now be improved.

A second concept of the JIT strategy is the demand-pull concept (see Fig. 4.7):

The demand-pull concept refers to the manner in which materials are "pulled" through the manufacturing process in the supply chain (Cheng and Podolsky 1996). The items necessary at one workstation are pulled from the preceding workstation only once required. This is very different from traditional manufacturing where items from one workstation are pushed onto the next one, regardless of whether the products are needed there or not.

Through the implementation of this approach, the proper use of JIT strategies for inventory and demand-pull, manufacturing has resulted in increased quality, productivity and efficiency, improved communication and decreases in costs and wastes. The potential of gaining these business benefits has made JIT a very attractive concept for manufacturing organisations.

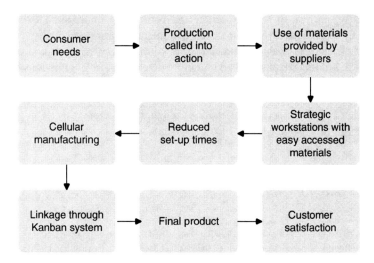

Fig. 4.7 The demand-pull concept in JIT
Source: Cheng and Podolsky 1996 Copyright ©

4.2.2   Elements of JIT Manufacturing

The JIT philosophy is holistic in its approach. It includes elements such as the human resources as well as manufacturing, purchasing, manufacturing, planning and organising functions of a business. If we group them along the Toyota manufacturing system methodology, we can look at the three elements:

- People
- Plant
- System

A JIT manufacturing system cannot be implemented successfully without the support and agreement from all the *people* involved. Therefore, employees as well as other stakeholders, such as shareholders, labour organisations, management and potentially also the government, need to be informed at an early stage. People will be more compelled to achieve goals when they are included in the development of such goals. JIT therefore tries to involve employees through the concept of total *people* involvement.

There are a number of changes in terms of manufacturing set-up that come with a JIT implementation. For example, under JIT manufacturing, the *plant* layout is arranged for maximum worker flexibility. The layout is arranged according to product rather than process. The concept of demand-pull manufacturing brings another important change within the *plant*. This concept involves the use of demand for a given product to signal when manufacturing should occur. This way, companies should only produce what is required in the appropriate quantity and at the right time. Lastly, the use of self-inspection and continuous improvement have to be adopted by each employee to ensure that mistakes and low quality work are corrected efficiently, goals and standards are continuously achieved and reviewed. Section 4.3.1 of this chapter will go into more detail regarding continuous improvement and quality goals.

Within a JIT organisation, the *system* refers to the technology and processes used to link, plan and co-ordinate the activities used in manufacturing. MRP as described previously in this chapter is one of such systems.

4.2.3   Limitations of JIT

Whilst a lot has been written about the numerous advantages of JIT, several shortcoming have been identified as follows (Cheng and Podolsky 1996):

1. Cultural difference – Since the JIT philosophy originated from Japanese culture and work ethics, it is suggested that JIT could be less successful in different cultural surroundings where resistance to change in attitude and worker philosophy exists.
2. Loss of safety stock – In traditional make strategies, large amounts of inventory are used as safety stock. Especially for companies with large spikes in demand, the elimination of safety stock to offset inaccurate demand forecasts can cause out of stock problems.
3. Decreased individual autonomy – Under JIT, employees must stick to strict methods of manufacturing in order to maintain the system. This in turn reduces the "entrepreneurial spirit" and individual autonomy of workers, which can become a major challenge for a JIT implementation.
4. Industry-specific success – JIT success may be industry-specific. It is suggested that craft-oriented businesses with a focus on assembly of products have performed better in JIT programmes, than organisations producing commodity type products.

To conclude, when looking at JIT programmes, it is important to acknowledge that certain limitations exist that could trade off the widely reported advantages of JIT in terms of increased quality, productivity and efficiency.

4.3   Lean Manufacturing

We have now covered how to set up manufacturing and how to make sure that it runs efficiently using the JIT approach. However, there is more in the make function than manufacturing planning and optimisation of its set-up. Important features of this function are to meet customer needs, work with reliable raw materials, ensure punctual distribution and minimise manufacturing mistakes. We therefore re-visit Mr. Ohno and his team at Toyota, to review their approach to quality improvement and waste reduction with the aim to improve manufacturing performance through lean thinking.

Lean thinking and lean supply chain strategies are all about using the right level of *man*, *machine* and *material* to produce what is required. Lean literally means "with no fat", thus focusing on the essential requirements for the manufacturing process. As a consequence, waste should be reduced as much as possible and *methods* and *machines* need to be optimised.

How can lean thinking improve the make process? First, we look at quality management and the philosophy of continuous improvement. Then, we identify where waste occurs in the process and what the adding value activities are. Lastly, we look at tools to reduce waste, sometimes referred to as "losses", and help improve the manufacturing process.

4.3.1 TQM and Continuous Improvement

Understanding quality and the power of continuous improvement is an important step when maximising manufacturing performance. Numerous books have been written about quality improvement approaches and philosophies (see end of this chapter for a selection of recommended readings). The biggest step change has been to move away from quality assurance, also called the "little q", and towards total quality thinking, also called the "Big Q" (see Fig. 4.8).

The *"little q"* represents the traditional quality and assurance attitude that used to be common in traditional businesses. This shift towards the *"Big Q"* represents the move away from simple quality control as an isolated business function, towards a more holistic approach that looks at all products, processes and services and improvement opportunities. Total Quality Management (TQM) builds on this approach of "Big Q" thinking and it can be defined as:

> A management approach for an organisation, centred on quality, based on the participation of all its members and aiming at long-term success through customer satisfaction, and benefits to all members of the organisation and to society. (Definition by ISO 8402:1994, later subsumed under ISO 9000)

TQM involves being proactive in performing the right activity, the right way, the first time and continuing to perform it to the required level. In manufacturing, this approach could translate into short manufacturing set-up times, material availability and high conformity to manufacturing plans. The TQM approach emphasises long-term benefits resulting from continuous improvements to *man*, method, *machine* and *materials*. Dealing with waste or losses plays an important role in the improvement process and will therefore be covered in the next section.

	Little q	Big Q
Focus	Manufacturing only	All products, processes and services
Scope	Technical concern relating to ultimate customer	Business concern related to all customers; internal and external
Attitude	Reactive after the event control Preservation of status quo	Proactive preventive approach Continuous improvement
What is waste?	Costs associated with deficient manufacture	All costs that would disappear if the right things happen right first time

Fig. 4.8 From quality assurance to total quality adapted from Truscott (2003)

4.3.2 Improving Performance Through Waste Reduction

Waste in the manufacturing process can be a lot of things: unused materials, defective finished goods, obsolete packaging, lost manufacturing time, uninformed operators and over-represented managers – the list of losses is potentially infinite. Waste is thus another term for inefficiencies or losses that can occur in the manufacturing process and in other parts of the supply chain and that need to be reduced as much as possible in order to improve performance. Activities, like counting stock, chasing orders, inspecting materials and moving finished goods into a warehouse do not add value but only add costs to the manufacturing bill. Therefore, in *lean manufacturing* these activities should be reduced as much as possible. Mr. Ohno and his colleagues have grouped typical wastes that occurred in manufacturing environments into the following seven categories:

1. Over manufacturing: production ahead of demand
2. Waiting: waiting for the next manufacturing step
3. Defects: The effort involved in inspecting for and fixing defects
4. Inventory: all components, work-in-progress and finished products not being processed
5. Motion: people or equipment moving or walking more than is required to perform the processing
6. Transport: moving products that is not actually required to perform the processing
7. Inappropriate processing: due to poor tool or product design creating activity

Each of these wastes should be reduced and if possible, eliminated in order to achieve improved performance results. If you are interested in a great novel on management philosophy and manufacturing improvements we recommend the book "The Goal" by Goldratt et al. (1993) who created the *theory of constraints* model for systems management.

4.3.3 Tools to Improve Make Performance

There are several tools to improve manufacturing performance. Most tools in this section centre on the elimination of losses and can therefore be seen as techniques for improving performance and efficiency. In this section you will learn how to draw a loss tree, how to conduct a 5-Why analysis and how to solve problems with a fishbone diagram.

4.3.3.1 Loss Tree Analysis

The loss tree is a process or tool to help you identify your priorities when aiming for quality improvements. It is used where there is more than one quality problem. A loss tree is a visual aid to identify where the issues are, it allows the user to focus on specific areas rather than generating a problem list. It also allows the user to benchmark the manufacturing performance against past data or competitors. The thinking behind drawing a loss tree follows the adage "if you don't measure it, you cannot improve it" (see Fig. 4.9).

Imagine that you are a production manager with L'Oréal. Your company invests a lot of time and money in measuring your current manufacturing performance and

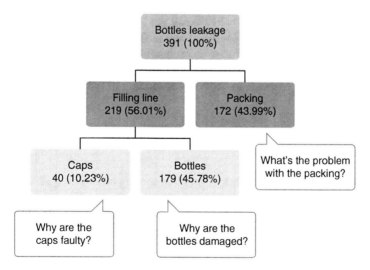

Fig. 4.9 Illustrated loss tree analysis example

analysing efficiency losses. One example of best practice is to improve the number of hair conditioner leakages on a production line. In this example, the analysis gave 391 leaking bottles per 1,000. Some of these losses were attributed to the filling line (219) and other leakages occurred during packing (174). The lowest level of the loss tree shows you that the majority of losses were found on bottles during the filling process. Therefore, the question "Why are the bottles damaged during the filling process?" may lead to your continuous improvement plan.

In TQM and continuous improvement, you will start with the biggest and work towards the smaller loss. This way, you can tackle the big problems with the large impact first according to the Pareto rule as described in Chap. 2 on Plan. As a consequence, you should be able to improve the current damage of bottles and therefore improve your overall manufacturing performance.

4.3.3.2 5-Why Analysis

This method of exploring the causes of problems by asking "why?" five times is called *"failure-cause"* analysis or *"5-why analysis"*, and it is a critical component of problem solving training delivered as part of the induction into the Toyota Production System (TPS).

This method builds upon the principle that the real cause can often be found as a result of repeating "why?" five times. Such exploration of causes should lead to improved methods to prevent recurrence. To conduct a 5-why analysis, information is taken from the fishbone analysis (see next section) and the issue summarised into a succinct statement.

The root cause of the problem, or the loss, is called the phenomenon in 5-why analysis. The possible reasons for the phenomenon are determined by examining the ideal conditions required to ensure a successful event. Each condition that fails is analysed closely by asking "why?" until the root cause is identified. From the answers gained actions can be identified and included in the improvement plan.

This is a simple structured root cause analysis technique. It is applicable to simple issues as well as complex problems with many variables. Its basis is in simple tenacity and demands in-depth understanding of the process being investigated.

4.3.3.3 Fishbone Diagram

The fishbone diagram is an effective problem-solving tool to be used by groups of people involved in finding the possible causes of problems. The cause can be split into the four categories we outlined earlier: *man, method, materials* and *machine*. Each of these categories is then examined in more detail and other potential causes added.

Let's have a look at an example fishbone diagram depicting possible causes for the loss in damaged bottles as introduced earlier in this section (see Fig. 4.10).

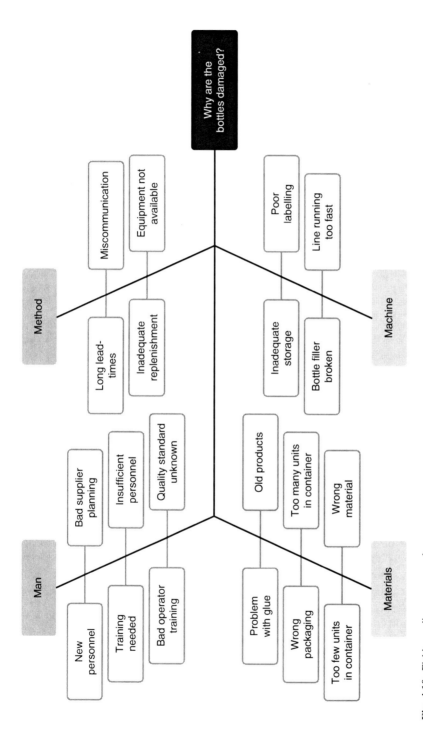

Fig. 4.10 Fishbone diagram example

This fishbone diagram shows that there can be many reasons why the bottles on the manufacturing line are damaged. It thus gives a complete overview of possible losses. For example, the hair conditioner bottles could have been damaged because the wrong material was bought. The bottle walls might be too thin to be handled by the machine and therefore get damaged in the filling process.

4.4   Case Study of Best Practice in Make: Unipart

Unipart rolls out lean manufacturing
The Unipart Group is an employee-owned international provider of logistics and manufacturing solutions specialised in lean manufacturing and the automotive sector.

The Assignment
Design and implement a lean programme in over ten factories in six countries for the world's leading manufacturer of welding products.

The Results
In the areas of focused effort the tangible benefits to the client included:

- 80% reduction in inventory
- 80% reduction in change over times
- 70% reduction in lead-time
- 20% improvement in quality
- 10% increase in productivity

The Unipart approach
A key task in this assignment was to design a way of introducing the most relevant lean tools into every factory within 12 months. These tools included: the visual monitoring of performance within teams; identifying and prioritising problems and issues and then solving them within the team in a structured way in order to deliver clear benefits and results.

The most difficult aspect of this challenge was to find a way of quickly engaging the operational people on the shop floor who had no previous experience of lean and whose first language was not English.

The solution was to deliver in all ten factories, minute by minute, day by day coaching to Production Managers and Team Leaders. Within 2 weeks Unipart constructed a highly skilled practical team of coaches drawn from the operations managers and team leaders within their own businesses. This group of expert practitioners was then each deployed into the various factories around the world, for a period of 4 months.

What did Unipart achieve?

(continued)

> During the 4-month period in each location, over 50 people were trained in problem solving, communication cells and workplace audits. Over 100 problems were identified with over 50 of these being solved at root cause and subsequent changes implemented. Forty problem-solving circles were completed and over twenty local facilitators were trained to enable this approach to continue. As a result, the improved operational effectiveness and efficiency enabled Unipart's client to improve its customer service to the extent that an external research company found that our client was regarded as the best welding consumables supplier on customer service in the world.
> Sarah Pickford
> Business Development Manager
> Unipart Manufacturing Expert Practices

4.5 Suggestions for Further Reading

Oakland, J. S. (2003). *TQM – Text with cases*, Oxford: Elsevier Butterworth-Heinemann.
Sheikh, K. (2003). *Manufacturing resource planning (MRP2)*, New York: McGraw-Hill.
Vollmann, T. E. (2005). *Manufacturing planning and control*, New York: McGraw-Hill.

References

Cheng, T. C. E., & Podolsky, S. (1996). *Just-In-Time manufacturing – An introduction*. London: Chapman & Hall.
Goldratt, E. M., Cox, J., et al. (1993). *The goal: A process of ongoing improvement*. Gower: Aldershot.
Plössl, G. W., & Orlicky, J. (1994). *Orlicky's material requirements planning*. New York: McGraw-Hill Professional.
Truscott, W. (2003). *Six sigma – Continual improvement for businesses*. Oxford: Butterworth-Heinemann.

Chapter 5
Guide to Deliver in Supply Chain Management

Abstract This chapter guides you through the deliver function of supply chain management and is split into three main sections. First, it looks at the components of deliver within supply chain management, describing distribution networks and their key trade-offs. Second, transport management and different modes of transportation are explored. Third, consideration is given to warehouse planning and different warehouse layouts. The chapter concludes with a case study of transport planning best practice in the company DHL.

Having read this chapter you will be able to:

- Explain the components of deliver in supply chains
- Define transport planning and operations
- Define warehouse planning and operations

5.1 Introduction to Deliver

The deliver function – sometimes also described as distribution management – is an integrated part of the end-to-end supply chain. In fact, one could say that deliver glues the different parts of the supply chain together. A useful way of thinking about this "glue" is the distribution network – a web of warehouses linking factories to customers (see Fig. 5.1).

The distribution network you see on the next page consists of three suppliers delivering materials into one factory. From the factory, finished products flow to three warehouses that in turn supply three customers. Companies constantly try to optimise their distribution network; the main aim is to reduce the number of warehouses in their network. However, consolidating warehouses does not come without problems. Most importantly, it increases the distance between the supplier and customer while decreasing responsiveness. This creates a key trade-off in our deliver set-up: balancing cost and service aspects.

Terminology in deliver varies. Some organisations refer to the deliver function as logistics, and in this book deliver is used interchangeably with distribution management. With respect to warehouses, different organisations use the term

C. Scott et al., *Guide to Supply Chain Management*,   75
DOI 10.1007/978-3-642-17676-0_5, © Springer-Verlag Berlin Heidelberg 2011

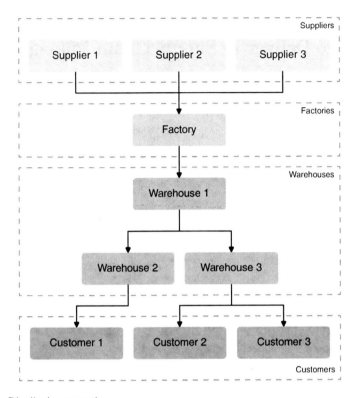

Fig. 5.1 Distribution network

depot or distribution centre (DC) instead. To simplify, this chapter refers to storage facilities as warehouses.

The deliver function is influenced by a number of factors, such as:

- Global economy
- Political decisions
- Advanced technology
- Environmental requirements

Transport and the world economy are closely linked. As manufacturing moves to different locations around the globe, this results in more product movements and increased transportation requirements. The challenge for the deliver function is to find solutions that follow the needs of a *global economy* with companies shifting from national to multi-country sourcing strategies.

Political decisions influence the deliver function on an equally large scale. The planning and construction of new roads, airports, rail links and seaports are often undertaken by national governments. Extending transport infrastructure demands large investments that usually require long lead-times and complex negotiations.

Another driving force for change in deliver is *advanced technology*. Radio frequency identification, global positioning systems, mobile telecommunication and satellites are but a few technologies that have already revolutionised transportation and warehousing. In the future, one can expect technology playing an even greater role.

Environmental requirements have grown in momentum. This has led to a number of environmental friendly innovations in the transport industry. Smooth paint, for example, reduces the water resistance of container vessels, which in turn reduces CO_2 emission in sea transport. Trucks now have aerodynamic features, which include new fuels and hybrid vehicles to reduce urban congestion. Conscious consumers strive for buying low cost products, but at the same time they don't want new ports and more airplanes spoiling the environment. This makes the deliver function a particularly interesting and challenging one.

5.1.1 Network Trade-Offs

Imagine a distribution network where every customer has its supplier warehouse next door. Lead-times from supplier to customer would be minimal, and customer service would be excellent. What would be the distribution network cost in this situation (see Fig. 5.2)?

As the number of warehouses increases, the associated deliver cost also increases because of three cost components (Chopra and Meindl 2010):

1. Facility costs
2. Inventory costs
3. Primary transport costs

First of all, the company would need to pay the warehouse running cost, such as insurance, labour and electricity, for each of the facilities. This is summarised in the *facility cost* curve.

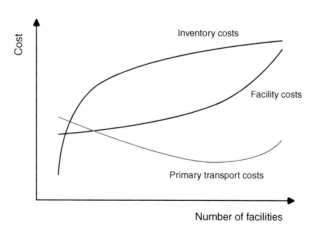

Fig. 5.2 Network distribution cost components

Secondly, *inventory costs* increase with every warehouse carrying additional amounts of safety stock.

Finally, *primary transport costs* are depicted in the third curve, which looks like a hockey stick. As we add warehouses to the network, primary transport costs first decrease because the transport distance gets shorter. If we keep adding distribution facilities to the network, the delivery quantity per warehouse becomes smaller and smaller, until trucks drive around half empty. This is the point where the primary transport costs curve goes up in the hockey blade; transport costs increase again.

5.1.2 *Facility Location Decisions*

Many supply chain companies consider changing their distribution network set up. Decisions to move, build or outsource new facilities in organisations involve significant investment and risk. When Hewlett-Packard bought Compaq in 2001, the company decided to reduce the total number of distribution facilities to reduce distribution costs. In order to work out the optimum number of facilities, Hewlett-Packard probably used one of the major network modelling programmes, Paragon being the most known one. These complex optimisation tools all work with the Centre of Gravity (COG) principles (McKinnon et al. 2002). With the COG method, you can locate facilities by using a weighting of customer demand data on a grid map. Mathematically, this method gives you the optimum location of your warehouse or distribution centre.

However, before the final network optimisation decision is made, other non-mathematical factors need to be considered, such as:

- Cost of commercial property in that location
- Availability of skilled labour
- Time to build or occupy the site
- Accessibility of government grant or subsidy
- Proximity of road, rail, water and air networks

It is tempting for an organisation to place a facility in a rural location as commercial property prices are generally lower compared to the urban equivalent. However, this location may have very little availability of skilled labour. When making facility location decisions, it is therefore best practice to start with a modelling tool and then add other considerations to the equation.

5.1.3 *Deliver Components*

There are three main components of deliver within supply chain management:

- Transport management: moving around products in trucks, ships, planes and trains

- Warehouse management: keeping and moving stock within depots, warehouses and distribution centres
- Order management: capturing the customer order all the way through to brining back a proof of delivery in order to raise an invoice

The rest of the chapter will focus on the first two components: *transport* and *warehouse management*. *Order management*, the third function of deliver, has strong links to customer service and inventory management, which you find covered in Chap. 2 on Plan and Chap. 10 on Customer Service.

5.2 Transport Management

In today's global supply chains, transport management has to be a very innovative and fast evolving part of business. Often its role is to make sure that products made in one part of the world arrive in full and on time in another part of the world, without sacrificing quality or exaggerating cost. Variables in transport management include:

1. Speed
2. Reliability
3. Security
4. Quality
5. Environment
6. Cost

Transport management can add value to global supply chain operations by offering different transport choices that perform differently on the six transport management variables. *Security*, for example, varies depending on the location and nature of the product to be delivered. In terms of *cost* impact, transportation cost contributes significantly to the overall cost of goods sold.

There are five different transport modes available for companies to choose from: air, road, rail, water and pipeline (see Fig. 5.3). Each mode has unique characteristics that satisfy different supply chain requirements. The choice of transport mode depends on the nature of the product and the specific requirements of the customer order.

Imagine that you are producing blue jeans for Levi Strauss & Co. in Asia. The jeans are sold in high volumes in the US. In this case, the *water* transport mode using sea freight might be preferred. This transport option has a very low per unit cost and the shipments are not time critical. A preferable option – when on land – would be using *rail* transport; this is a particularly cheap and secure transport mode.

Now imagine that you are acting on behalf of De Beers Group, a famous diamond trading company. The diamonds are mined in South Africa and sold in Belgium. In this case, the *air* transport mode using airfreight may be preferred as the product demands high security standards and a short lead-time.

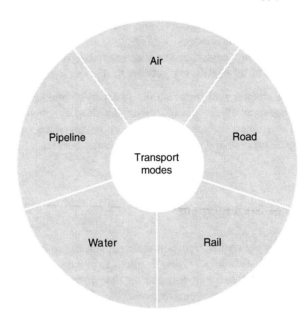

Fig. 5.3 Different modes of transport

An important factor to consider is that transport modes can compete with each other. As air transport networks expand and the airfreight unit cost falls, both *road* and *water* lose volume. With the innovation of refrigerated containers, *water* has taken volume of fresh produce from *air* and *road*. For example, fruit and vegetables arriving to Europe from overseas can now be shipped as sea freight.

5.2.1 Air

There are three options for transporting goods by air:

- Cargo operators
- Courier operators
- Niche operators

The bulk of global airfreight takes place using *cargo operators*. These are usually line-haul operators who specialise in cargo. An example is Cargolux, an operator with its head office in Luxembourg. Cargolux is one of the largest scheduled all-cargo airlines in Europe with a global network; they fly with a fleet of 16 aircrafts to over 64 destinations. There are also operators who run a mixture of passenger and cargo operations, such as China Airlines or Cathay Pacific. Cargo is often carried in Unit Load Devices (ULDs) that can come in the form of pallets or containers. These air cargo containers are generally made of aluminium and come in a small range of standard sizes. Some air cargo containers may have additional features such as refrigeration.

Courier operators carry goods in parcel format. Global providers of these air express services include TNT Express, UPS, Federal Express and DHL. Operating their own fleets of aircraft, these courier companies typically fly all parcels out of national or regional airport hubs.

Niche operators engage in air transport services that are neither offered by cargo nor courier operators. Niche operators are often run by military-related agencies; they transport large goods and vehicles, such as heavy equipment and tanks, by air. However, special aircrafts that transport large parts of the Airbus A380 aircraft from France to Germany would be an example for non-military niche operators.

5.2.2 Road

Road transport offers "door to door" transport flexibility through Full Truck Loads (FTL) and Less than Truck Load (LTL) options. Road tonnage per kilometres has increased greatly in recent times and is still increasing around the globe as India and China become wealthier. Road transport can be split into two categories:

*   Primary transport
*   Secondary transport

Primary transport vehicles are large and generally used in upstream supply chains. Primary transport takes raw materials or finished products from ports, airports, rail terminals, factories or warehouses to a distribution centre. A typical size load in primary transport would be 40 ft. in length (12,192 mm).

Secondary transport, in comparison, picks up customer orders from the distribution centre and delivers them to the customer. Secondary transport vehicles will generally be smaller trucks, vans or even motorcycles in order to deliver customer orders effectively in urban areas. Some secondary transport operators use hybrid vehicles to reduce inner-city congestion.

5.2.3 Rail

The next mode of transport, rail, is excellent for high-density products over long distance and suitable for low-value, non-time-sensitive deliveries. The downside to rail transport is that transport routes are limited to fixed-track and terminal facilities, which may differ in gauge size when railing internationally. Rail is a major player in intermodal transport and can provide "piggyback" services, such as:

*   Trailer on Flat Car (TOFC)
*   Container on Flat Car (COFC)
*   Rolling Road Train (RRT)

In *TOFC*, a truck driver drops a loaded trailer after driving it by road to the rail dock. The loaded trailer is placed on a flat rail car and then transported over long distances to its destination. The trailer will be unloaded, and a second truck driver will pick up the trailer and deliver it to the customer.

COFC is similar to TOFC, but instead of a trailer it involves a container – coming from a sea terminal or road depot – loaded on a railcar. With COFC, double staging of containers is often used to optimise rail load efficiency.

In *RRT,* an entire road train drives on a flatbed rail car. RRT is often used in the automotive industry to transport new cars from the factory to car dealers. After arriving at the final rail terminal, the road train drives off the flatbed railcar and continues the delivery by road. With RRT, the load keeps moving while the driver takes the rest breaks required by law. The Channel Tunnel between England and France in Europe is an example where RRT takes place frequently.

5.2.4 Water

Water transport encompasses the following main activities:

- Tankers: carrying products like oil and Liquid Natural Gas (LNG)
- Container vessels: carrying standard and refrigerated containers
- Inland waterways: boats and barges using canals and river networks

Modern maritime shipping evolved from a historic "tramp"-shipping basis, where vessels used to operate like a taxi service with no fixed routes or schedules. Nowadays, shipping lines operate more similarly to a bus service with set routes and set sailing schedules.

Tankers carry different liquid products, the main ones being crude oil, chemicals and LNG.

Container vessels emerged after an important transport invention by Malcolm McLean in 1937: the container. These large ships can be up to 400 m long and hold as many as 15,000 containers.

Inland waterways have always been used as a long distance transportation method. Some countries rely heavily on inland waterways such as India, which has about 14,500 km of navigable waterways.

5.2.5 Pipeline

Pipeline is the last mode of transport and despite it being an important one, pipeline is often forgotten when it comes to transport choices. Hundreds of thousands of kilometres of pipeline carry oil and gas "invisibly" every day for our world's energy consumption. Only products with certain specifications – liquid, gas or powder – can be pushed under pressure and in large volumes through pipelines. The initial infrastructure investment in pipelines is very high and can have important social and political consequences.

5.2.6   Intermodal Operations

Intermodal operation describes the transport of goods using two or more different transport modes. When these goods cross international boundaries on their journey to customers, six factors become important (see Fig. 5.4).

Let's consider an example where the supplier is the Indian-based manufacturer Whirlpool, the customer is the US retailer Wal-Mart and the transport provider is the Danish shipping company Maersk.

To keep cost and service at an optimum during this long product journey, the shipping company needs to possess extensive *SCM knowledge* – in this case Maersk.

As the washing machines move from India to the US, many different transportation modes and vehicles will be used. These *physical assets* need to be owned by the shipping company or a contracted supplier in order to make this journey happen.

Washing machines are sold every day by Wal-Mart and thus products need to flow on a daily basis. Although Maersk may not own some of the transport assets, *operations management* is critical for constant product supply. Daily operations could refer to daily loading at the Indian sea terminal or maritime operations sailing the white goods to the US.

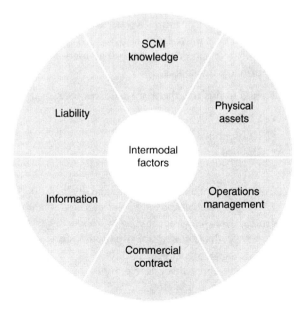

Fig. 5.4 Intermodal factors

Due to the international nature of most inter-modal operations, the *commercial contract* needs to be in place to align transport rates and agree payment terms and currencies.

Information is vital to ensure products arriving safely at its destination. A track-and-trace information system may tell Wal-Mart the exact location of the load on its journey from India. Track-and-trace systems can also be used to tell customs at the US port of destination what the value of the load is. This way, import tax can be paid quickly.

Finally, *liability* is a crucial factor to agree before engaging in intermodal operations. In international trade, international commercial terms (Incoterms, see also http://www.incoterms.com) are used to clarify who is liable at each moment during the journey.

5.3   Warehouse Management

The warehousing function creates a clearly defined break point between supply and demand in supply chain management (Grant et al. 2006). The term "warehouse" can be substituted by many similar terms, such as:

- Depot – often used in the context of transport vehicle management, e.g. a train depot
- Facility – refers to a factory or a warehouse building
- DC – Distribution Centre, where warehouse and transport activities take place
- RDC – Regional Distribution Centre
- NDC – National Distribution Centre
- Transhipment centre – a warehouse that holds product orders for short periods while they move from vehicle to vehicle
- Hub – a national centre often used for warehousing, administration and primary transport

To add to this list, there are different formats of warehouses, such as:

- Contract
- Refrigerated
- Bonded
- Cross-docking

Contract warehousing is managed by a third party and is discussed further in Chap. 11 on Outsourcing. *Refrigerated* warehousing provides temperature-controlled storage while *bonded* warehousing is under custody of a government body: the products stored are usually tax duty unpaid. *Cross-docking* warehouses carry no safety stock but hold bulk stock of orders that enter and leave the warehouse within a short time period.

The aim of warehousing is to achieve an optimum position between minimising the total cost of operation while providing the desired service level for the business.

In setting out to achieve this basic aim, warehouse management needs to consider the three major constituent elements of labour, space and equipment. These three elements will reflect the total cost of any warehouse operation. The level of service provided to customers will be determined through the processes and procedures used to receive, store, pick and dispatch the products from the warehouse. The physical nature of any warehouse operation makes it labour intensive, requiring a high level of man-management and control, which results in increased costs. Balancing the cost and service trade-offs in warehouse management is challenging. Similar to transport management, technological support from computerised control systems make warehouse management an innovative, fast changing and exciting part of the supply chain.

5.3.1 Warehouse Planning

When planning warehouse operations, it is important to be aware of the expected development of products, volumes, suppliers and customers. These are all essential for warehouse management in order to plan the necessary resources and where these should be located over the long term.

The reasons for setting up warehouses are similar to the reasons for holding inventory (see Chap. 2 on Plan): warehouses are there to provide a secure location for products closer to our customers and to build up safety stock to buffer against uncertainty in demand. Warehouses also provide us with additional benefits: they function as a shelter for goods and a hub for road distribution.

Planning the number and locations of warehouses is important in SCM as it impacts the cost-service trade off significantly. Warehousing normally represents about one-third of the total distribution cost of a business with labour and space; warehouse operations cost amounting to about 90% of the costs and 10% for equipment. The productivity and procedures managed within theses warehouses then dictate the costs, service, quality and time outputs that provide value for customers.

In warehouse planning it is important to achieve the optimum combination of:

1. Maximising storage space in cubic terms
2. Minimising handling operation

To help achieve this, it is beneficial to use a warehouse planning process.

5.3.2 Warehouse Planning Process

The warehouse planning process is a management tool that can be used to plan the construction of new warehouses or to optimise the running of existing warehouses (see Fig. 5.5). The first step is to *assess the inventory*. This will provide a profile of the inward and outward movements. It also provides the basis for the *calculation of the space*, which will be required to store all products. Next, the *warehouse layout* can be planned and sketched. This will allow distances to be calculated and the

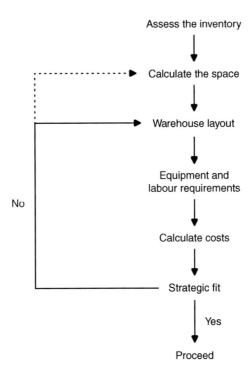

Fig. 5.5 Warehouse planning process

equipment and labour requirements can be determined. The *calculated costs* are reviewed and compared with the total budget available. If the warehouse planning project shows *strategic fit* with the business strategy, then the optimisation or construction of a new warehouse can *proceed*.

If the warehouse plans and business strategy do not align, the planner has to return to the top of the process to calculate space, and then different choices of work method and equipment will need to be recalculated. This can be continued until the required result is reached.

5.3.3 Warehouse Layout

There are four main activities within the warehouse layout:

1. Receipt
2. Storage
3. Picking
4. Dispatch

The natural flow of goods through the warehouse is represented by these four stages. When planning the warehouse, we should try to shorten the distance of

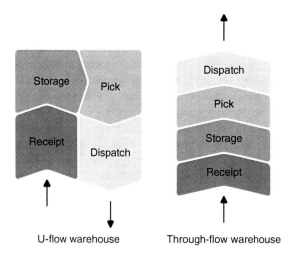

Fig. 5.6 Warehouse layouts and flows

travel from one to the next and make the movement as smooth and continuous as possible (see Fig. 5.6).

There are two main warehouse flow systems (see Fig. 5.6). A *U-flow warehouse* has the loading and receiving docks next to each other on one side of the building. This means that docks can be allocated for loading and unloading as required. The U-flow warehouse can be extended on three sides of the building if necessary. Vehicle parking and access as well as personnel and equipment can be shared. With only one main gate, the U-flow can be easily managed and secured.

A *through-flow* layout shows receiving and dispatching docks at opposite ends of the building. The through-flow system is often used when goods received are from an adjacent manufacturing source, or when different vehicles are used for unloading and loading of goods.

5.4 Case Study of Best Practice in Deliver: DHL

An integrated planning solution for temperature-controlled road transport operations
DHL Supply Chain (DHL) provides solutions to customers around the globe. This case study considers an integrated planning solution for DHL customers that produce chilled and frozen food and need it transported to their customers by road transport.

(continued)

What was the situation before?

DHL was operating six site operations for customers who supply temperature-controlled goods to large supermarket chains, smaller retailers and the food service industry. As part of the ongoing relationship with DHL, the team in this case identified that the customers had similar products going to similar destinations using the same mode of transport.

As each of the six sites operated independently it was clear that there could be an opportunity to achieve benefits if these six operations were planned as one, and integrated together under one roof. For example if there were two transport planners in each site, that would mean 12 planners were being used in total. If an integrated solution was implemented where the planning was managed in one location, this number could be reduced and benefits could be obtained. However, an obstacle to streamline the operations was poor visibility of the overall road transport network operations as they all ran independently. Also, due to sickness leave cases and absenteeism, there was a risk of skill and manpower shortage in transport planning.

What changes took place?

DHL set up a new single control tower for the planning of their temperature-controlled business. The control tower manages all the planning, compliance with road transport legislation, customer service and administration. Staff were relocated and recruited to run the control tower. The six operations were then set up to manage the onsite driver activity and the successful execution of the control tower produced plan.

The control tower was not just desks with PC's on top. A state of the art space was created with plasma screens, video walls and the latest systems to create an excellent working environment as well as having the ability to track vehicles and produce live up to date KPI information.

What were the challenges?

Finding the right space was a challenge. It was key not to have "just another office". It was difficult to get people to relocate and also to recruit people with the right skills all in the one location. As a result there was a learning curve experienced during the launch phase of the control tower. The systems were the same but had to be used differently. This linked to the processes that needed to be adjusted to fit the integrated as oppose to a fragmented planning model. The team used the DHL DePICT Project Management methodology to reengineer the processes now used in the control tower today.

What are the positive results?

There is now an integrated planning solution in place that has improved customer service, costs and visibility as well as carbon reduction. In terms of customer service, there is a dedicated team with allocated roles to support the customer. There is greater visibility of the whole operation to allow clear information flow to improve service. Costs are improved as the integrated

(continued)

solution reduces empty miles, also helping with the green logistics agenda. Also there is better sub-contractor procurement and management due to the economies of scale.

By ensuring a core number of staff present in the control tower at all times, overall management is facilitated and holiday or absence gives less risk exposure.

There are new opportunities as a result; for example integrating the retail outbound (supermarket) deliveries with the DHL inbound deliveries. As the control tower has excellent road transport visibility it can now identify retail delivery vehicles from other DHL contracts and reroute them to collect from its own six operations. In this way service, cost and green credentials are further improved.

Paul Farr
General Manager European Control Tower
DHL Supply Chain

5.5   Suggestions for Further Reading

Emmett, S. (2005). *Excellence in warehouse management: How to minimise costs and maximise value*. Chichester, West Sussex: John Wiley & Sons.
Frazelle, E. (2001). *World-class warehousing and material handling*. New York: McGraw Hill.
Lowe, D. (2009). *The transport manager's and operator's handbook*. London: Kogan Page
Ramberg, J., Rapatout, P., Reynolds, F., & Debattista, C. (2000). *ICC guide to incoterms 2000 – Understanding and practical use*. Colorado: ICC Publishing.
Ross, D. (2004). *Distribution planning and control – Managing in the era of supply chain management*. New York: Springer.

References

Chopra, S., & Meindl, P. (2010). *Supply chain management: Strategy, planning and operation*. NJ, Pearson Prentice Hall: Upper Saddle River.
Grant, D. B., Lambert, D. M., Stock, J. R., & Ellram, L. M. (2006). *Fundamentals of logistics management*. London: Irwin/McGraw-Hill.
McKinnon, A., Button, K., & Nijkamp, P. (2002). *Transport logistics*. Cheltenham: Elgar.

Chapter 6
Guide to Return in Supply Chain Management

Abstract This chapter guides you through the return function of supply chain management. First, it helps you to understand the importance of reverse logistics, its drivers and key players. Second, the return process will be discussed in detail and different return business models will be depicted. Third, it will explore a strategic outlook of returns, along with examples from different industry sectors. This will include trends in reverse logistics and the golden rules to improve returns performance will be highlighted. This chapter concludes with a case study of best practice on recycling operations within the company Wincanton.

Having read this chapter you will be able to:

- Explain what the return function is and how it fits into the supply chain
- Describe the return process with its product discovery options, process stages and the business models of ownership
- Recognise industry trends and their implication for return

6.1 Introduction to Return

Return describes the process of returning logistics for goods, packaging material and transport equipment. This encompasses customers, retailers, manufacturers and suppliers. In the SCOR model, return can be found at each interface between supply chain partners, all the way from the suppliers' supplier to the customers' customer.

In the supply chain examples discussed in the previous chapters, the focus was on moving goods downstream to meet customer demand. Now, in the return supply chain, we are exploring product travelling the opposite way – essentially sending products back to where they came from!

The term Reverse Logistics (RL) is often used in conjunction with returns management in supply chain literature. "Going the wrong way on a one-way street" (Lambert and Stock 1981: 19) was one of the first definitions of RL. Although organisations use these terms differently, we will use return and reverse logistics interchangeably in this chapter. Reverse logistics can be further defined as:

...The reverse process of logistics (Krumwiede and Sheu 2002: 326)

...An organisation's management of material resources obtained from customers (Jones 1998: 619–620)

...The process of moving product from its point of consumption through channel members to the point of origin to recapture value or to ensure product disposal (Schatteman 2003: 267)

The above stated definitions represent the traditional view on reverse logistics where the emphasis lies on the backward supply chain. A more holistic and modern definition would also include processes and activities to *avoid* returns, to reduce materials in the forward supply chain (so that fewer materials flow back) and to ensure the possible reuse and recycling of materials.

Drawing on the European Working Group for Reverse Logistics' definition, we define reverse logistics as:

The process of planning, implementing and controlling backward flows of raw materials, work-in-progress, finished goods and information, from the point of consumption to the point of recovery or proper disposal.

The term "green logistics" is often mentioned in conjunction with reverse logistics (see Fig. 6.1).

Whilst those two terms overlap there are certain areas and activities that are more associated with reverse or green logistics respectively (Rogers and Tibben-Lembke 2001). Whereas RL is mostly commercially oriented, green logistics summarises logistics activities that are primarily motivated by environmental considerations. These environmental considerations could result in designing products with waste-reduced packaging. Also practices and technologies that lead to lower levels of CO_2 and noise emission form part of green logistics, as well as choosing transportation modes depending on their environmental impact (see also Chap. 5 on Deliver).

Reverse logistics

• Product returns
• Marketing returns
• Secondary markets

• Recycling
• Remanufacturing
• Reusable packaging

• Packaging reduction
• Air & noise emission
• Environmental impact
  of mode selection

Green logistics

Fig. 6.1 Comparison of reverse logistics and green logistics adapted from Rogers and Tibben-Lembke (2001)

6.1.1 Why Do Products Return?

There are several reasons why products are returned in the supply chain. According to Schatteman (2003) the most common reasons for returning a product are:

- Customer is not satisfied
- Installation or usage problem
- Warranty claim
- Faulty order processing
- Retail overstock
- Manufacture recall program

Most retailers and manufacturers allow the return of a product within a certain period after purchase if the *customer is not satisfied*. Such money back guarantees have become standard practice for direct sales channels including catalogue sales and purchases online. There is, however, the risk that consumers abuse this money-back guarantee by ordering and then returning a new product they simply wanted to try with no real intentions of keeping it.

When customers experience *installation or usage problems* of a recent purchase, they might perceive the product to be defective and therefore return it to the manufacturer. This difficulty in set-up or installation is common in the computer industry where some products, such as CD-ROM drives, have a very high return percentage. In order to avoid the extra cost of falsely returned products, manufacturers should keep installation procedures for end consumers as simple as possible and include clear first use instructions.

In some product categories, it is common to send back defective products to retailers or manufacturers for repair. These *warranty claims* can occur immediately after purchase if the product received is faulty on arrival or cosmetically damaged. Alternatively, products might break down during the course of their life cycle. Typical product categories with warranty are consumer electronics, as well as household appliances such as washing machines and vacuum cleaners.

Another reason for product returns can be *faulty order processing*. An error in order entry or processing can cause shipping problems for consumers or retailers where the shipment does not arrive on time and in full. Common issues can include late delivery, incomplete shipments or wrong quantities. In those cases, customers can make a claim against the manufacturer and return the entire or part of the shipment. Error-free order processing is especially important before seasonal or special events such as Easter or Christmas where deliveries are often time critical. If companies do not have effective order processing they expose themselves to funding customer errors.

Manufacturers can grant retailers the luxury of returning unsold stock after a certain period of unsuccessful sales. This practice can be important to improve the retailer's cash flow and to clear space for new stock in the shops. Sometimes, this practice is abused by the retailer to make accounting figures look good at the end of the quarter or month and then to reorder the same stock at the beginning of the next month. Sending back goods because of *retail overstock* is common practice in the book industry. Seasonal products such as sun lotions are also returned to the manufacturer at the end of the summer. Once a product has reached the end of its life cycle, many manufacturers prefer to get the product off the shelves to prevent cannibalisation with the new version. There are two options with end of product life cycle or product replacements: Either the manufacturer takes back the stock based upon the agreed conditions with the retailer or the retailer disposes the old version himself and requests a credit note.

A last reason why products are returned might be a serious flaw in the quality of the product, triggering a *manufacturer recall program*. Recalls appear more often in the automotive, pharmaceutical and toy industry where product safety is extremely important. In order to limit damages in such situations, discredited products need to be moved quickly out of circulation and into designated storage centres. From there, the manufacturer decides whether to replace certain parts of the defective product, or whether to dispose it entirely.

Alongside these reasons for product return, Krumwiede and Sheu (2002) outline a number of terms commonly used with returns management and operations (see Fig. 6.2).

6.1.2 Drivers of Reverse Logistics

There are three main drivers that have led RL to become part of many senior managers' strategic agendas:

- Legislation
- Economics
- Corporate citizenship

6.1.2.1 Legislation

In many countries, governments have introduced regulations on how to handle products in the supply chain in order to protect the environment. The European Union has been a leader in developing regulations such as the End-of-life Vehicle directive (ELV) and the Waste Electrical and Electronic Equipment Directive (WEEE) legislations.

These legislative reforms have led to an extended producer responsibility. In some industries, manufacturers are now obliged to take back and recover their products after use, in order to reduce volumes of waste disposal. This is especially true for certain product groups, such as household appliances, automobiles and electronics.

In the US, the Environmental Protection Agency (EPA) emphasises the important and integral role of "re-manufacturing", to reduce energy consumption and

Term	Definition
Product Recalls	Goods the manufacturer has recalled and must be picked up for return.
Inventory Returns	Goods returned to reduce inventory at an outlet other than the manufacturer.
Warranty Returns	Goods a store/distributor/wholesaler knows are in need of warranty return.
Core Returns	Reusable goods; those items that can be remanufactured.
Reusable Containers	Shipping containers that product was shipped in and must be returned.
Damaged Goods	Goods damaged in shipment or damaged on site.
Seasonal Items	Items returned due to the end of a season, which causes the item to have no retail value in the next season(s).
Hazardous Materials	Items considered hazardous and yet must be returned; also known as HAZMAT.
Stock Adjustments	Goods transported to correct a situation where there is an abundance of items at one location and lacking in other locations.

Fig. 6.2 Returns terminology
Source: Krumwiede and Sheu (2002), Elsevier

waste. Therefore smart companies are not waiting passively to be forced into legislative compliance. Instead many manufacturers have developed "green" supply chain practices. The five Green Supply Chain Management (GSCM) practices according to Klassen and Johnson (2004) include:

- Environmental certification, e.g. product specific eco-labels or ISO 14001
- Pollution prevention
- Life cycle assessment – to quantify the environmental burden and impact throughout a product's life
- Design for the environment – also termed green product design

As can be seen from this list, reverse logistics is an integral part of green supply chain practices.

Some companies are already preparing for the next generation of environmental legislation, when the producer might be made fully responsible for the disposal of the end of its useful life. Thus, they are actively rethinking the producer's role, responsibilities and opportunities in reverse logistics.

6.1.2.2 Economics

RL programmes may bring two types of economic benefits:

1. Direct gains
2. Indirect gains

Direct gains from RL can mean significant financial benefits in terms of cost, revenues and Return On Capital Employed (ROCE) for the manufacturer. The recovery of materials is often cheaper than building or buying new materials. Examples include product groups such as copying machines, computers, aviation equipment and tyres, where manufacturers such as Xerox have started to reuse old parts in new products for economic benefits (Jayaraman and Luo 2007). Metal scrap brokers have been able to build successful businesses by collecting metal scrap and offering it to steel works. Steel works are interested in metal scrap because they can mix it with virgin materials in their production process and thus reduce their production costs. Effective RL can also minimise the cost of environmental compliance and waste disposal.

In addition to reduced costs, increased revenues can be achieved. In consumer goods, the selling of fresh stock is more profitable than the selling of unsold or slow-selling stock at a discounted level. For example, millions of Easter chocolate eggs are sold in the UK in the weeks before the Easter holidays in spring. The time window for Easter eggs is quite short, and after the holidays, the chocolate eggs can only be sold at a discounted rate. Thus, in order to maximise the profitability of this Easter business, the eggs need to be distributed quickly to the right retailers. Some areas might sell quicker than others, so reverse logistics and a redistribution of eggs can support smooth sales and reduce obsolete stocks. Through effective RL, companies can avoid markdowns on older products by managing inventories in such ways that fresh stock is always available. Since fresh stock sells at a higher retail price, an increased turnover can be achieved.

Re-manufactured products can often be sold in secondary markets producing an additional stream of income, whilst utilising existing technology and assets. Returns can also yield valuable information about product performance, merchandising effectiveness and product line profitability. In that way, company efforts can be streamlined and resources can be used more effectively. Companies can thus maximise their ROCE.

Indirect gains in RL often relate to marketing, competition and strategic actions. Taking back products can be used as an image building operation. Customer might reward green supply chain practices with greater customer loyalty leading again to increased revenues. It can also be used to strengthen relationships with customers or suppliers by collecting feedback together with the returned product. RL can thus be developed as a competitive advantage.

High competition exists from online retailers and TV shopping networks that generally employ generous return policies. The power has shifted towards retailers and customers who demand high standards in returns policies. Therefore, the competitive pressure to liberalise retailers' and manufacturers' return policies drives reverse logistics. Satisfied end-consumers and retail customers have become an important asset in logistics operations. Thus, taking back unwanted products to increase customer satisfaction has been employed as a strategic driver in reverse logistics.

6.1.2.3 Corporate Citizenship

Companies use the term corporate citizenship to express that they respect society out of good principles. In the context of reverse logistics, corporate citizenship describes a set of values or principles that drives a company to start engaging in reverse and green logistics. Philanthropy and goodwill returns can help to portray good corporate citizenship.

Nike's *Reuse-A-Shoe* program where old athletic shoes are being collected and turned into sports surfaces for community use can be viewed as an example of major success in corporate citizenship. The program was started in 1993 as an effort to show the company's environmental and social responsibility. Since then, more than 22 million pairs of old sports shoes have been collected and transformed into about 300 sports and playgrounds around the world. Through this program, Nike does not only take responsibility for the recycling of their products, but they also promote their commitment to increase physical activity of young people through building new community sports grounds. This project has led to an improved company image and potentially will help the company to increase sales of sport shoes in the future.

Companies are often involved with reverse logistics for a mix of legal, economic and social driving forces and it is sometimes hard to set the boundaries. Many companies issue Corporate Social Responsibility (CSR) reports in addition to their annual financial reporting to outline their corporate citizenship and sustainability efforts. Returns management and RL make a substantial part of the CSR reporting picture, as the Korn/Ferry Institute on global and green supply chains points out (Millen and Walker 2008).

6.1.3 Key Players in Reverse Logistics

According to Blumberg (2005) and De Brito and Dekker (2003), a larger number of different groups show significant interest in the management of RL:

- Forward supply chain companies (e.g. high-tech and consumer oriented manufacturers) that must provide RL services as part of their business practices to comply with the legislation, retrieve economic gains or show corporate citizenship
- Specialised reverse chain players and 3rd Party Logistics (3PL), e.g. recycling specialists, waste and junk dealers, that are active in the collection and processing of parts and waste, and that are concerned with potential market opportunities
- Governmental institutions (e.g. the European Union and national governments) that introduce new legislation and issuing directives with the aim of waste reduction and ecological sustainability

Vendors, developers and consultants of technology, infrastructure and software for managing reverse flows are also interested in the growing area of RL practices. This part of the industry is growing and there is a need for specialised services and technology.

6.2 The Return Process

6.2.1 Reverse Logistics Activities and Recovery Options

The return process starts with the injection of a used product from the point of consumption, back into the supply chain. There are some basic product recovery options in returns management that can be employed after the used product has been returned (see Fig. 6.3).

These product recovery options and their definition are:

- *Resale*: Immediate selling of returned products such as catalogue returns or customer lease to secondary markets
- *Repair*: Bringing damaged components back to a functional condition
- *Reuse*: Using good components from retired assemblies (mostly spare parts) for refurbish or remanufacture of products
- *Remanufacture/refurbish*: Restoring a product to a like-new condition by reusing, reconditioning and replacing parts
- *Recycle*: Taking component materials and processing them into useful material
- *Scrap*: Disposal of products if no alternative course of action is available

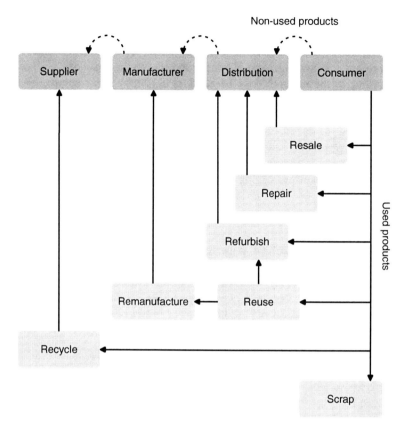

Fig. 6.3 Product recovery options
Source: Kumar and Putnam (2008), Elsevier

The choice of the recovery option as outlined depends on the composition, deterioration and use-pattern of the returned product. A product that is relatively easy to disassemble, e.g. a car, might be entered into more recovery activities than a product that is difficult to separate into its different streams of materials, e.g. a sports shoe.

6.2.2   Five Stages of the Product Return Process

The product returns process can be broadly split into five stages covering the receive, sort and stage, process, analyse and support steps of the return process (Stock et al. 2006: 61).

6.2.2.1   Stage 1: Receive

During the first stage of the reverse logistics process, product returns are received at a central location. Returned items may include a wide assortment of products that are returned via different carriers in packages, on pallets or in individual containers. This first step, to receive returned products, requires much more flexibility and complexity handling in comparison to most forward supply chain activities. At this stage, a return acknowledgement is printed and sent to the customer.

According to the research done by Stock et al (2006), some companies find it most effective to make a disposition decision at this stage. This is similar to the postponement strategy in forward logistics, where a value added service is performed as close to the customer as possible. The company can avoid processing expenses for items that are truly worthless, as well as turn around items quickly that are ready for resale. However, in reality most companies make their final disposition decision only after sorting, staging and processing (stages 2 and 3 in the process).

6.2.2.2   Stage 2: Sort and Stage

Once an item has been received, it has to be sorted for future staging in the returns process. This sorting can take place according to the format of return, the type of return or size of item being returned. In most companies, the first two steps of receiving, sorting and staging returned items takes 3 days or less, with many companies having standards of 1–2 days.

6.2.2.3   Stage 3: Process

The items are sorted according to their SKU number or vendor number. Having the appropriate information on the return label of the product allows for items from the same customer to be processed at the same time. At this point, customer credits for the returned items can be given and the paperwork that accompanied the return is separated from the item and sent to the administration area.

6.2.2.4   Stage 4: Analyse

Employees working at the fourth stage of the process, the analyse stage, must be the most highly trained in reverse logistics as they have to decide for the most appropriate recovery option. Extra care and resources should be dedicated to motivating and constantly enhancing these employees' professional skills and abilities (Genchev 2009).

Since the value of the returned item varies depends on the chosen recovery option, individuals working here must be aware of the financial impact and benefits associated with each option. For example, returned mobile phone with a weak battery pack that can be repackaged for resale will return greater financial gains than items that have to be refurbished or remanufactured. Items that are scrapped and disposed have the lowest remaining value.

Secondary markets for resale, refurbish, and repair items should be treated just like any other market: with an understanding of customer needs, price elasticity and effective channels of distribution. The success and the profit margin of the company engaging in the RL process will depend partly on the effective marketing of these re-activated products.

6.2.2.5 Stage 5: Support

When the disposition of the product has been chosen, the item will be distributed according to where it should go. For some of the recovery options, the product will go to a repair centre close to the distribution centre. For other options, the returned product will be sent back to the manufacturer.

Because recovery rates for repaired and refurbished are relatively high compared to remanufactured or recycled products, performing repair and refurbish efficiently at low cost is important to a company's return on investment. The cost includes transport, storage and handling, as well as labour for the actual exchange of parts. Whereas labour is cheaper in some regions it may not pay off to move products too far away from the markets because of added transportation cost and reduced value over time. Interestingly, British Airways decided to utilise an overseas operation for returning misplaced customer luggage during the launch of the London Heathrow Terminal 5. Getting items ready for resale quickly can reduce inventory-carrying costs. From a service perspective, the sooner these items are made ready for resale the higher the customer service levels, especially for items where demand is high and safety stock has been used up.

To conclude, the more efficient and timely each of these five stages in product returns is performed, the greater the profitability of the RL operations and the higher the return on capital employed.

6.2.3 Different Return Business Models

There are three main ways to run RL supply chains (see Fig. 6.4).

The term *closed-loop* describes the process where used materials or products are returned and processed by the manufacturer and thus the same party that is responsible for the forward logistics. Closed-Loop Supply Chains (CLSC) is thus one of the business models used in reverse logistics where the manufacturer organises the full five-stage process of RL. Examples of CLSC include IBM, Xerox and Canon. The advantages of operating a CLSC can be found in the direct and indirect economic benefits discussed earlier in this chapter, as well as the control that the manufacturer keeps over the product flows. By keeping RL in-house, the manufacturer can protect the products' design and Intellectual Property (IP) and take closer care of certain sensitive or highly valuable components. Another benefit is the customer service that is enhanced through the closed-loop processes. Customers in the heavy equipment industry might prefer to buy

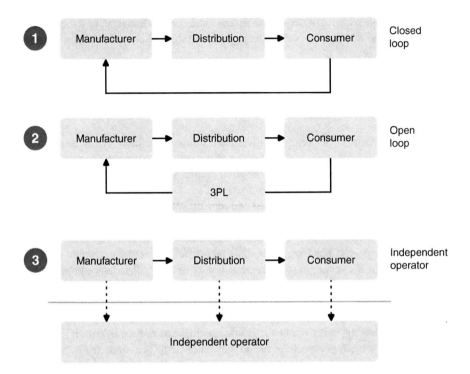

Fig. 6.4 Three return business models
Source: Kumar and Putnam (2008), Elsevier

a complete life-cycle package of warranty and service, rather than having to deal with a number of product, service and warranty providers separately.

When manufacturers do not operate the reverse flows themselves we speak of *open-loop* models. The manufacture might decide to outsource its returns to a 3PL provider that is specialised in a particular product group. This provider then handles the reverse logistics function including maintenance, repair and return of products on behalf of the manufacturer. For example, Roadway reverse logistics handles Hyundai core-reusable parts for the remanufacture of transmissions from Hyundai dealers. This outsourced business model operates on a profit-sharing basis where the gains of the repaired, refurbished and resold products are split between the 3PL and the manufacturer.

The third business model in RL supply chains is called *independent operators* that function completely outside the forward supply chains of Original Equipment Manufacturers (OEMs). These operators are mostly traditional waste and junk dealers or service organisations. Independent operators can be run as a business or as a governmental service. Their emphasis is on the economic disposal and recycling of products and packaging.

The choice of business model depends on the type of industry, the available product recovery options and the residual value of materials involved.

6.2.4 Product Recovery Issues

Although there are excellent examples to be found globally of product recovery, it is important to recognise the general issues that could occur in the product recovery industry (see Fig. 6.5).

The product recovery sector is largely *unorganised* in comparison to the traditional manufacturing and forward logistics sector. Only a few of the remanufacturing and recycling companies operate with formal contractual relationships with their suppliers or their customers. One of the reasons behind the unorganised sector is the relatively immature state of the remanufacturing industry. The high volatility and associated risk act as a barrier to become more established and organised.

A *lack of information and skills* can also be observed. For many products, it is rather time-consuming to obtain design information, an indication of the residual product life as well as the end-of-product-lifecycle value. This information is required in order to make good product recovery decisions. The cost and effort of information retrieval is often not justifiable due to the low-value nature of returned products. Specific skills are required for inspecting and evaluating products at the analysis stage. Skilled employees need to be present locally as shipping returned products to a central location would deteriorate product margins even further. Hence, the absence of "readily available" information as well as local competence can hinder efficient returns operations.

Whilst the traditional manufacturing industry is demand driven, i.e. the industry operates to meet customer demand; the remanufacturing industry operates on a *supply driven* basis. The RL process starts when an end consumer or retailer injects

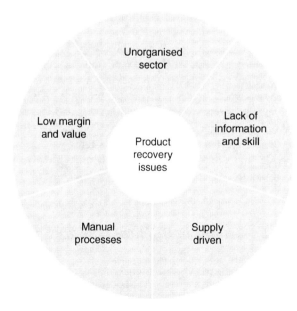

Fig. 6.5 Product recovery issues

a product into the reverse supply chain, where the timing, quality and quantity of these product returns is very difficult to forecast. Thus, the remanufacturing company has very little control over this supply-driven rate of returns.

Despite the advance and automation of production processes in traditional industries, reverse logistics operations are mainly conducted using *manual processes* along the five stages as explained earlier in this chapter. This makes the product recovery process generally slow, expensive, error-prone and inefficient. One of the biggest obstacles against automation is the lack of flexible tools that could support this very specific industry.

The majority of players in the product recovery industry operate on very *low margins*. These margins are further challenged through time-sensitive items, such as clothing, books and consumer electronics. In these industries, any delay in product returns causes a significant reduction in market value leading to lower margins. Therefore, low margins due to the rapid value depreciation in the product recovery industry can be another barrier.

6.3 Strategic Outlook in Returns

To start with a few industry examples, product return rates vary according to the types of retail and industry (see Fig. 6.6).

Very high return rates can be found in publishing and electronics industries. It is estimated that overall, customer returns make up 6% of all product returns across the retail sector (Rogers and Tibben-Lembke 2001).

De Brito and Dekker (2003) reviewed 60 case studies and found that around 60% of all returns were in manufacturing. In the wholesale and retail trade, about 20% of products were returned and 10% in construction. The remaining 10% were spread over various industries. With regard to the products and materials involved, almost half the cases dealt with were metal products, machinery and equipment. Around 30% of the products being processed in reverse logistics were transportable goods such as wood, paper and plastic products. Around 20% were food products, beverages, tobaccos, textiles and apparel and less than 10% fell into the category of ores and minerals. The majority of the cases involved high value products.

It is expected that product return rates will grow because of legislation, economic and corporate citizenship drivers. Finally, the increasing use of home delivery through the Internet sales channel has a very high return rate.

6.3.1 Returns in Different Industry Sectors

Different industries have handled returns in different ways. In some industries, end-of-life returns have been strongly regulated by governments for a long period, including the following industry sectors:

Industry	Percent
Publishing (magazines)	50%
Publishing (books)	20-30%
Distribution (books)	10-20%
Manufacturing (computers)	20-30%
Printers	18-35%
Auto industry (parts)	10-20%
Consumer electronics	18-25%
Household chemicals	4-8%

Fig. 6.6 Sample return rates by sector adapted from Rogers and Tibben-Lembke (2001)

- Automotive
- Electronics
- Appliances

Reverse logistics practices have the longest tradition in the *automotive* sector. Due to the value of steel, aluminium and other components, this sector has the most advanced recycling processes compared to the electronics and appliance industries. The ELV is aimed at preventing and managing waste that is associated with the automotive industry. In some countries, the responsibility for appropriate disposal lies with the consumers. In other countries (like those of the European Union), the responsibility is shifting towards the producers. As a consequence, producers in the automotive industry in Europe are aligning with independent operators such as dismantlers and recyclers, to improve disassembly starting at the design phase and moving forward through the supply chain. The biggest challenge for the automotive industry when it comes to the ELV implementation in Europe is the international scope that this industry operates in. Consequently, foreign producers who do not have disassembly information or reverse supply chain networks may have to transport vehicles back to the country of origin or pay higher fees (Kumar and Putnam 2008). Also, it is likely that US and Asian vehicle producers will be at a disadvantage compared to European manufacturers such as Volvo or BMW, who are already engaging in very efficient dismantling designs. BMW's strategic aim is to offer cars that are designed for complete disassembly. The vision is to take back used cars from the consumers via car dealers, disassembled them and then put back the parts into the forward manufacturing stream for new cars.

In the *electronics* industry, the challenge is to be successful both from an ecological as well as an economic perspective. For Europe, WEEE is the driving legislative force in this industry. However, economic profit from remanufacturing and recycling has not yet been yielded for many consumer products due to high labour cost for dismantling, little automation and lack of recycled material markets.

In addition, few products are designed for easy disassembly and there is a concern that competitive advantage could be lost by publishing component make-up for disassembly or recycling (Kumar and Putnam 2008). On the other hand, companies such as Xerox, Kodak and Electrolux have taken on board corporate citizenship for reverse logistics, which can provide a case of best practice for other players in the industry.

Appliance products, such as refrigerators, cookers and washing machines can have a field life of 7–16 years, which makes the rate of return and end-of-life value hard to predict. Similar to the electronics industry, few manufacturers have perfect information and visibility on their components' chemical make-up and also here few products are designed for easy disassembly. However the similarities with the electronics industry, the recycling process of appliances is more similar to vehicle recycling because of the metal, CFC refrigerant (in cooling appliances) and motor recovery (Kumar and Putnam 2008). Thus, the appliance industry has the opportunity to leverage existing collection and recovery processes and coordinate improved economic savings in the disassembly and recycling process by taking the more advanced automotive reverse logistics industry as a role model.

6.3.2 Improving Returns

Manufacturing companies are moving through the twenty-first century knowing that developing faster, more efficient and cost-effective reverse logistics processes will be of competitive advantage. According to Jones (1998), there are three activities that companies can do to increase their return efficiency:

- Design for disassembly
- Recycle more material
- Increased product lifecycles

Whether producing cars or baby prams: many manufacturers are investigating ways to design their products with *disassembly* in mind. Traditionally, manufacturers strove for the most efficient assembly method. Now they design their products to such ways that they are easily pulled apart for reuse, recycle or scrap.

Many traditional industries are looking for ways how to *recycle more material* in the manufacturing process. The incentive for investigating into this area often comes from environmental legislation, but direct and indirect economic gains are being sought as well. Scrap dealers already extract 95% of the main metals in cars (aluminium, steel, copper and brass) and sell those materials into secondary markets. Lately, the re-use of water bottles and tetra pack material has become more common in the manufacturing of pens, carrier bags and other everyday items.

With the aim of *increased product life cycles*, the trend also goes towards the use of modular design and manufacturing techniques, where out-of-date components can be easily upgraded. The iPhone is one of the first mobile phones where technology upgrades can be pursued through software rather than having to exchange the hardware.

6.3.3 Golden Rules for Returns Management

There are golden rules for improved reverse logistics management. The authors Jayaraman and Luo (2007) provide three insights on how to best compete in an industry in which a new value chain strategy needs to be redefined urgently according to the authors.

First, returns must be treated as perishables: Every delay in transporting, sorting, processing and repacking of returned printers, for example, reduces the value remaining in the product.

Second, value chain partnerships in reverse logistics are crucial. Specialised 3PL providers can often handle tasks such as credit issuance and product disposition much more efficiently than manufacturers.

Thirdly, returns can provide valuable customer feedback. A well-managed reverse supply chain allows the manufacturer to retain contact with the customer and gather valuable feedback from them. This customer feedback can be used to adapt the product mix and to correct any failings in product design and distribution infrastructure.

6.4 Case Study of Best Practice in Return: Wincanton

Comet and Wincanton Recycling manage WEEE together

Wincanton Recycling is a transport and warehousing company that specialises in end-of-life electrical returns. This way, Wincanton helps manufacturers and retailers to comply with the WEEE directive that came in place in Europe in 2006.

Comet is the second biggest electrical retailer in the UK, after the market leader DSG International – the electrical retail group that owns retail brands like Currys, Dixons and PC World. Comet's electrical equipment like kitchen appliances, refrigerators and TVs are sold and delivered through their home delivery network; some of which is run in-house and some of which is run by a third party. Like their competitor DSG International, Comet offers a returns service. When Comet delivers a new refrigerator to the customer's home, they offer to take away the old one.

Setting up return operations

In 2005, Wincanton Recycling commenced their first national sorting and re-use contract with Comet. The aim was to form a WEEE partnership between the two companies while integrating outbound and return operations to achieve the following three aims:

1. To reduce Comet's carbon footprint
2. To utilise existing infrastructure wherever possible
3. To embed Wincanton Recycling with Comet's operations

(continued)

In the beginning, when Wincanton Recycling was just setting up its new customer Comet, Wincanton's returns fleet was operating stand-alone but running in parallel to Comet's outbound operation. That meant that two vehicles were going to the same household and back: The first one to deliver the new refrigerator, and the second one to pick up the old refrigerator for re-use. This initially led to increased transportation cost and an increased number of trips to be co-ordinated.

Wincanton suggested to change this initial set-up and to use the outbound fleet for returns as well. As a consequence, Wincanton Recycling moved their recycling platforms – four in total across Britain – closer to Comet's two main regional distribution centres and started streamlining the logistics operations.

Tackling operational challenges

When embedding the returns flows into the outbound fleet, Wincanton Recycling had to work very closely with all of its customer's outbound delivery platform managers to make this change happen. In this process, some operational challenges had to be tackled.

For example, the differences between outbound and returns fleet equipment had to be considered. As all of Comet's outbound vehicles were double deck trailers, finding a method of loading both decks of the vehicle with return heavy household appliances was something Wincanton Recycling needed to work on.

Another challenge was the co-ordination of outbound and returns traffic at Comet's small outbound home delivery platforms. Wincanton had to be careful not to clog up the platforms with returned goods. Therefore, Wincanton started monitoring the return collection performance making sure that Wincanton would clear the platforms quickly by moving the goods on to its own recycling platforms.

Managing WEEE together

After having overcome these challenges, Wincanton now runs a two-tier sortation process with its customer: Comet picks up the old refrigerator and brings it to the home delivery platform where a simple sortation and inspection will be performed. At this first stage, anything that is in a fairly good condition will be refurbished and repaired by Comet. Anything that is classified as end-of-life at this stage will be sent onto one of Wincanton's four recycling platforms. Here, Wincanton Recycling re-sorts the goods. Products for re-use will be sent on to one of the recycling plants, and the remaining goods will be disposed.

Today, the outbound delivery fleet does 90% of the returns movements. Wincanton and Comet are now in their second contract term.

Looking into the future

In the future, Wincanton Recycling would like to move from end-of-life operations further upstream in their customer's reverse supply chains. Wincanton's aim is to become the sole reverse logistics partner with more retailers like Comet. It is predicted that there will be a lot more emphasis on

(continued)

highly sophisticated reverse logistics solutions making a link between returns and point of sales. This trend will be particularly true for high quality and more expensive product streams, e.g. home cinema systems, and Wincanton Recycling wants to be part of it.

Euan Jackson
Managing Director
Wincanton Recycling

6.5 Suggestions for Further Reading

Rogers, D. S., & Tibben-Lembke R. S. (1998). *Going backwards: reverse logistics trends and practices*. Reno, NV: Reverse Logistics Executive Council.

References

Blumberg, D. F. (2005). *Introduction to management of reverse logistics and closed loop supply chain processes*. Boca Raton, IL: CRC Press.

De Brito, M. P., & Dekker, R. (2003). *Managing reverse logistics or reversing logistics management?* Erasmus Research Institute of Management: Rotterdam.

Genchev, S. E. (2009). Reverse logistics program design: A company study. *Business Horizons, 52*(2), 139–148.

Jayaraman, V., & Luo, Y. (2007). Creating competitive advantages through new value creation: A reverse logistics perspective. *The Academy of Management Perspectives (formerly The Academy of Management Executive) (AMP), 21*(2), 56–73.

Jones, T. (1998). Reverse logistics, bringing the product back: Taking it into the future. In J. L. Gattorna, R. Ogulin, & M. W. Reynolds (Eds.), *Strategic supply chain alignment – Best practice in supply chain management* (pp. 619–632). Brookfield: Gower.

Klassen, R. D., & Johnson, P. F. (2004). The green supply chain. In S. New & R. Westbrook (Eds.), *Understanding supply chains: Concepts, critiques, and futures* (pp. 229–251). Oxford: Oxford University Press.

Krumwiede, D. W., & Sheu, C. (2002). A model for reverse logistics entry by third-party providers. *Omega, 30*(5), 325–333.

Kumar, S., & Putnam, V. (2008). Cradle to cradle: Reverse logistics strategies and opportunities across three industry sectors. *International Journal of Production Economics, 115*(2), 305–315.

Lambert, D. M., & Stock, J. R. (1981). *Strategic physical distribution management*. Homewood, IL: RD Irwin.

Millen, J. & Walker, L. L. (2008). *The 21st century supply chain executive: Global and green* (pp. 2–8). Los Angeles (CA). The Korn/Ferry Institute.

Rogers, D. S., & Tibben-Lembke, R. S. (2001). An examination of reverse logistics practices. *Journal of Business Logistics, 22*(2), 129–148.

Schatteman, O. (2003). Reverse logistics. In J. L. Gattorna, R. Ogulin, & M. W. Reynolds (Eds.), *Handbook of supply chain management* (pp. 267–279). Aldershot: Gower.

Stock, J. H., Speh, T., et al. (2006). Managing product returns for competitive advantage. *MIT Sloan Management Review, 48*(1), 57.

Chapter 7
Guide to Strategy in Supply Chain Management

Abstract This chapter guides you through the topic of strategy in Supply Chain Management (SCM) and is split into three main sections. First, it introduces corporate strategy in organisations and defines competitive strategy. Second, it considers how SCM can support a competitive strategy and how organisations can align their supply chain strategies. Third, it explains concepts that can support supply chain strategy development, in terms of the key drivers, ways they can decouple supply and demand, and what choices they have for lean and agile strategies. The chapter concludes with a case study of best practice for supply chain strategy in the company Wal-Mart.

Having read this chapter you will be able to clarify:

- Corporate and competitive strategy in companies
- Strategic alignment in supply chain companies
- Concepts to support supply chain strategy development

7.1 Introduction to Corporate Strategy

The first part of this guide has considered supply chain management from functional perspective, what supply chains are and how they operate. The second part of the guide will consider a strategic view of supply chain management before looking at the impact on the other key activities in particular people, finance, customer service and outsourcing.

7.1.1 What is Corporate Strategy?

Corporate strategy is *the direction and scope of an organisation over the long term: ideally, which matches its resources to its changing environment, and in particular its markets, customers or clients so as to meet stakeholder expectations* (Johnson et al. 2008: 10). Some key terms used when discussing strategy are shown (see Fig. 7.1).

C. Scott et al., *Guide to Supply Chain Management*,   111
DOI 10.1007/978-3-642-17676-0_7, © Springer-Verlag Berlin Heidelberg 2011

Fig. 7.1 Terms used in
strategy adapted from
Johnson and Scholes (2008)

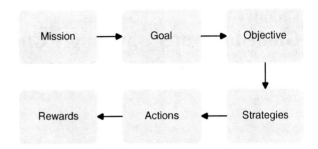

The *mission* describes the purpose of an organisation. An example would be Novartis, who offers a wide range of healthcare products through pharmaceuticals, vaccines and diagnostics. Their mission statement reads: "We want to discover, develop and successfully market innovative products to prevent and cure diseases, to ease suffering and to enhance the quality of life". The overriding focus in the whole of the Novartis business should fit their mission.

A *goal* is the aim or purpose. A goal could be: "To grow business revenue or to give increasing returns to our shareholders". The goal needs to be substantiated by the objective. Good examples could be

- To build bottom line profit by 10% every year for the next 5 years
- To launch five €1 million turnover new products in the next 3 years

Defining the *objective* is not easy as it needs to be really clear, measurable and needs a verb included so people have to do something. If it is totally unrealistic people will give up and it needs to have time parameters set so people can work towards them.

Strategies are then considered, the broad types of actions that will be needed to achieve the objectives. The *actions* are the specific activities by team or individual and lead to the *rewards*, the payoff for satisfying the objectives.

In summary all organisations are faced with the fact that they need to continually manage their strategies and there are many successful and less successful examples of this taking place. An example would be IKEA that has become one of the world's most successful companies over recent decades because of the way it has defined a clear customer focus, clear long-term strategy and implemented that strategy. However IKEA is aware that the strategies it has adopted over time might not be successful for the next decades. Kodak was very successful in the photographic industry for many years, but did not have a strategy to keep it at the forefront of the digital photographic age. It has now reinvented itself to align to the rapidly changing marketplace.

7.1.2   What is Competitive Strategy?

Implementing an effective competitive strategy can be the key to business success. The importance of this competition was highlighted by Porter (2004) and also by

Fig. 7.2 Competitive strategy

Treacy and Wiersema (1997). By integrating their teachings Fig. 7.2 gives an insight into how supply chain organisations can compete.

Different companies will seek to achieve a competitive advantage in the market place in one of the three generic strategic options. It may be possible to utilise two of these options and very rarely all three. They can be summarised below as:

- *Operational excellence*: delivering high quality products quickly, error free and for a reasonable price.
- *Customer intimacy*: delivering what customers want with high service and superior value.
- *Product leadership*: delivering products and services that push performance boundaries and delight customers.

An example of *operational excellence* could be Procter and Gamble; end consumers use their hair products in large volumes, the quality is good and they are reasonably priced.

The hotel chain Ritz Carlton may focus on *customer intimacy*, where their customers don't expect to pay a low price or to have the latest innovations in their hotel rooms, but do want to be recognised by staff when they arrive and enjoy a superior customer value experience.

Finally *product leadership* could be in the computer or telecoms industry, for example Apple and Nokia. These companies don't have the cheapest products in the market or perhaps the best perceived service, but they have the latest products that astound their customers, for a short period at least, until new products are released.

In summary, organisations make decisions about their competitive strategy and once made then need to consider how their internal structure will deliver them.

7.2 Achieving Strategic Alignment in Supply Chain Companies

There is a link between an organisation's competitive and functional strategy (see Fig. 7.3).

To execute the *competitive strategy*, the different functions within an organisation must develop and operate supporting plans and strategies. The *product development*

Fig. 7.3 Linking competitive and functional strategy

strategy identifies the portfolio of products that a company will develop and the functionality that they will have. It will also specify whether these products will be internally or externally manufactured.

The *sales and marketing strategy* segments the market and identifies the product structure and how it will be positioned, priced and promoted.

The *supply chain strategy* specifies how materials will be sourced, where and how the production activity will be performed, where and how deliver and return will be operated and how the customers will be supported after delivery.

To implement a competitive strategy successfully, it is vital that all the functional strategies are integrated together to ensure that they are complementary. It may be useful to consider the different strategies as a system and not mutually exclusive. They all need each other and in turn, support each other in their journey to success.

Strategic alignment is achieved when the competitive strategy and the supply chain strategy have the same end goal. It refers to consistency between the customer priorities – those that the competitive strategy is designed to satisfy and the supply chain capabilities – those that the supply chain strategy aims to build.

7.3   Concepts to Support Supply Chain Strategy Development

There are many methods available for strategic decision-making within the supply chain. For this guide we will consider three that are topical in product companies with whom the authors have worked. The first of these is to segment our supply chains using the four drivers of supply chain performance. These drivers are inventory, information, facilities and transport. The second concept examines the decoupling point position or strategic inventory, where supply and demand meet in the supply chain. The third explores the concept of lean and agile strategies before the final concept of a postponement strategy is considered.

7.3.1   Four Drivers of Supply Chain Performance

The model of the four drivers of supply chain performance proposes a structure that supports the supply chain strategy (Chopra and Meindl 2010) (see Fig. 7.4).

The strategy for each of the four drivers should be considered and decisions made how to best satisfy the supply chain strategy. *Inventory* decisions, which are covered in Chap. 2 on Plan, include what cycle or safety stocks should be held, where and in what quantities.

Information includes decisions on systems requirements, for example how should we run our MRP systems. This was discussed in Chap. 2 on Plan. Information would also include technology requirements, for example Internet, to give the required capabilities.

Facilities include both manufacturing and warehouse strategies and would consider the strategic location or capacity requirements.

Transportation decisions are covered in more detail in Chap. 5 on Deliver and include mode and network decisions. Therefore in summary, the four drivers of supply chain performance can be used as tool to provide a structure to support the supply chain strategy.

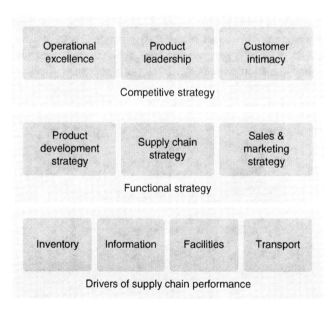

Fig. 7.4 Drivers of supply chain performance

7.3.2   Five Inventory Strategies

A different perspective for supply chain strategy can be gained by considering the supply chain as a combination of processes. The supply process is the upstream activity, whilst the demand process is the downstream activity. The buffer between the two is normally the major inventory point. Let's consider the tea supply chain from Chap. 1 again to view this point in the chain (see Fig. 7.5).

The demand process is driven by customer orders and this "pulls" the product through the supply chain. The supply process is driven by a forecast with the intention of providing the "push" for the product to the stock point in anticipation of future demand. You can also refer to this major inventory point as the "decoupling point", since it "decouples" the order and forecast driven activity. There are five inventory strategies that are used depending on the market requirements and product characteristics (see Fig. 7.6).

Let's start at the very right: *1 – Make and deliver to stock* occurs when the customer places their order and it penetrates into the supply chain to the point where stock is held. The stock is removed and sent to the customer to satisfy the order. All of the activity to the left of the decoupling point is designed to replenish the stock of product. A typical example of this would be a retailer of consumer goods like Carrefour, Wal-Mart or GAP that holds stock in all their retail stores.

In the *2 – Make to stock* model, the stock has been moved further upstream, usually into some form of central holding, for example a single regional warehouse. A typical example would be an Internet retailer such as Amazon or a mail order company holding central stock. Customer deliveries are executed from this central stock holding point.

Now we move onto *3 – Assemble to order,* where the stock point has been moved even further upstream. No stocks of finished goods are held, as the stock point simply comprises of work in progress material. When the customer places an order it penetrates into the supply chain as far as the stock point. Upon receipt, final assembly is then scheduled and once completed it is shipped to the customer.

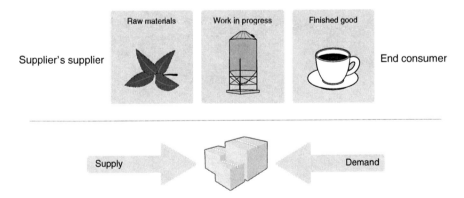

Fig. 7.5 Major inventory point

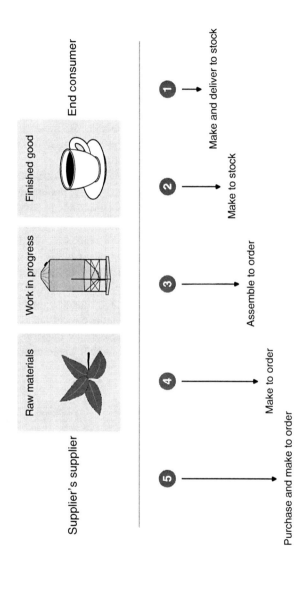

Fig. 7.6 Five inventory strategies

Dell computers operate this model via its Internet sales channel. This is the world of mass customisation where cars are made from stored components tailored to our requirements. McDonald's restaurants also operate this model in quiet customer demand times. Interestingly at busy times they can no longer satisfy the customer lead-time by assembling to order, so shift the model to make to stock for this period.

Now we see the stock point being moved further upstream in the *4 – Make to order* model. Here only stocks of raw materials are held. On receipt of the customer's order, the manufacture of components is planned and then the final assembly to allow the product to be shipped. Examples of this model could be customised kitchen furniture and jewellery.

In the final model, *5 – Purchase and make to order* the supplier holds no stock. When the customers order is received the product is designed, the raw materials ordered, production and assembly planned to enable the product to be shipped. Shipbuilding or specialised bridge building is a good example of this model.

The five models represent significantly different ways to operate a supply chain. Choosing the location of the decoupling point will also determine the performance profile of the supply chain. Let's now return to the concept that the decoupling point represents the separation of order driven activity from forecast driven activity (see Fig. 7.7).

There is an essential difference between these two types of activity. Order driven activity is based upon the known requirements of the customer. Usually this means that we are managing certainty. There can be situations, particularly when the decoupling point is located upstream, when the requirements are known. On the other hand forecast driven activity is an attempt to manage uncertainty. Usually historical demand is used in conjunction with mathematical techniques to project the pattern of demand into the future. Whilst attempts are made to reduce forecast error it is highly unlikely it will be totally eliminated. Customers requiring short

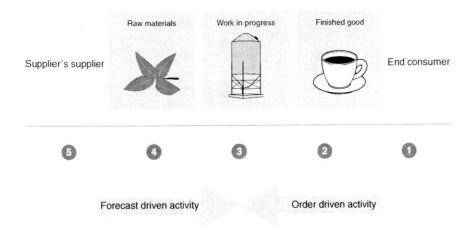

Fig. 7.7 Order and forecast driven activity

lead-times pull us towards a decoupling point downstream. If we can move back upstream costs can be reduced and service potentially improved.

The decoupling point position will be determined by a trade-off analysis considering the cost and service implications. The outcome of the analysis is one of the most important strategic supply chain decisions, since it will form the basis for how the supply chain is structured.

7.3.3   Lean and Agile

Historically, the supply chain for fashion retailers was to manufacturer in Asia, a long way from the customer and use slow, long lead-time sea freight with high inventories. Now, successful fashion retailers, for example Zara, manufacture close to their customers in more expensive but more agile operations that are more aligned to the competitive strategy. Considering the above two example supply chains, specific terms can be used to describe these two different approaches, lean and agile. A lean supply chain is trying to supply demand at lowest cost. An agile supply chains is trying to respond quickly to demand. Thus we can distinguish between two supply chain strategies (see Fig. 7.8).

Some organisations may be best operated with a lean strategy where products are more easily forecasted and purchased in high volumes over long periods of time. Or an agile strategy is required where each product launched has either very high or very low sales over a short product lifecycle. There is a danger that organisations have a

Lean supply chain strategies	Agile supply chain strategies
Maximise performance at minimum product cost	Use postponement
Lower margins because price is a prime customer driver	Higher margins as price is not a prime customer driver
Lower manufacturing costs through high utilisation	Maintain manufacturing capacity to allow response to uplifts in demand
Minimise inventory to lower cost	Maintain safety stock to meet unexpected demand
Shorter lead time but not if it creates higher cost	Reduce lead times even if cost is involved
Suppliers based on cost and quality	Select suppliers based on speed, flexibility and quality
Low cost modes of transport	Responsive (expensive) modes of transport

Fig. 7.8 Comparison of lean and agile strategies

"one strategy fits all approach". If we continue to do this we lose competitive advantage as we underserve our agile customers and overcharge our lean customers.

Paint mixing in hardware stores traditionally involved holding finished goods inventory at retail level. This results in low variety, high stock and potential obsolescence. A different strategy would be to have a lean supply chain for forecasted components (white paint, empty tins in only a few standard sizes). As soon as the customer orders the supply chain switches to agile using an under-utilised machine to very quickly mix the paint for the customer. Again McDonald's restaurant chains that agilely convert lean components on receipt of an order have a similar lean to agile strategy in this context.

7.3.4   Postponement

Most retailers have no choice but to hold finished goods in their shops near their customers. Most of the shops we use have to be at make and deliver to stock. If they tried to be at purchase and make to order, all the shelves would be empty and you would simply walk out and buy your food or clothes elsewhere.

We know from our decoupling point understanding that as we move from upstream in our decoupling point, our costs reduce and service increases, provided we can still manage the customers' lead-time expectations.

Postponement is one method to achieve this and can be defined as *"delayed configuration based on the principle of common platforms where the final assembly or customisation does not take place until the final market destination and/or customer requirement is known"* (Christopher 2005: 216).

Let's discuss the example of Benetton, the Italian textile manufacturer and retailer to illustrate the concept of postponement. The retailer's textile goods are made and stored as finished goods in Italy using the make to stock model. They are then distributed to numerous other European countries and held in distribution centres. The retail outlets in each country call off the textiles on a weekly cycle and store them in their shops waiting for customers to purchase the products. Essentially this is now a make and deliver model. This caused large issue with:

- Inventory value – money tied up in producing finished goods of textiles
- Variety – Benetton had 2,000 different combinations of sizes and colours of textiles in Italy, in European distribution centres and in the retail outlets
- Obsolescence – due to fashion changing quickly there was huge wastage

To counter these issues the decoupling point position was analysed. Although the retail organisation had to remain at make and deliver in its shops, it reconsidered the make to stock strategy at the distribution centres. Benetton decided to employ a postponement strategy by moving the textile dying (colouring) operation from the Italian factory to each European distribution centre. Suddenly, the factory held no more finished goods stock and the distribution centres simply dyed the textiles according to the shops orders on a weekly basis. The factory and distribution centres held the un-dyed textiles (only 40 varieties) and at the last minute in the supply chain these were converted into the finished goods (2,000 varieties). This helped to reduce inventory investment, by reducing the variety until order driven and therefore reducing the risk of obsolescence.

7.4   Case Study of Best Practice in Strategy: Wal-Mart

Innovating fresh produce supply chain through International Produce Limited (IPL)/Wal-Mart model
IPL is a unique supply chain strategic model within the sector of fresh produce products. The model is focused on controlling the supply chain with four key benefits:

- Improved shareholder return
- Reduced cost to the consumer
- High quality products
- Sustainability for the growers

It started as a joint venture between two companies: Bakkavor and Thames Fruit, owned by the grower Emilio Theresa. The success of this over 5 years led to IPL being bought by the Asda/Wal-Mart group.

Traditional model
In a normal supermarket supply chain, you have supermarket buyers or traders, in contact with importers. The importers will then buy from exporters anywhere around the world, and these exporters will buy from growers. Consequently there are a number of different people involved in the chain all collecting their margin.

Added to that is the logistical cost, i.e. the cost for warehousing and transportation. In the case of fresh produce, a significant amount comes from South Africa and South America by temperature-controlled reefer transportation.

New model
In the new model, IPL takes out the middlemen. Therefore Asda directly engages with the growers and exporters. There are two different inbound flows: the products either go direct to an Asda distribution centre, or goes to one of the two IPL sites. The UK sites are situated in Normanton near Leeds and in Spade Lane near Sittingbourne – both in the UK. Here, the product is picked, packed and sent to the DC's.

Cost reduction strategy: postponement of pick and pack
In the beginning of the project, everything was about how much of the product do you get packed direct at source – as this was the perceived cheaper option than packing in the UK.

(continued)

But actually, this supply chain approach did not go well with the requirements the supermarkets had in terms of changing size pack forms and the total
logistics costs. These now are balanced carefully against the reduced packing
costs, if sourced outside of the UK.

When the products are packed, they must immediately have their shelf life
displayed on the packaging. Hence the later the product is packed, the more
options the supply chain can utilise. Additionally, if the product is packed
later downstream, the decision on pack size form is postponed until the
demand is more certain which gives more flexibility.

With regard to the total logistics costs, when you ship loose plums,
960 kg can be accommodated on a pallet; if you punnet (the packaging
format for the consumer) and then ship, you can only get approximately
630 kg on a pallet. Immediately, everything you might save from a cheaper
packing price might be lost as you transport packaging around the globe
with no added value. An additional benefit of postponing the packaging is
that there is an improved product quality recovery ratio. This is because if
some poor quality fruit is detected in a punnet – the entire punnet should be
destroyed. Whereas if detected in a loose shipment, the single fruit can be
isolated and removed.

Quality strategy: vertical integration of quality control

Each DC has an Asda Quality Control (QC) presence on site: They work
together with IPL, to make sure that all fresh produce leaving the depot is in
the right quality condition. The benefits are clear: Rather than sending
products to the stores and getting them back as a rejection, QC on site inspect
stock before sending it out and therefore reducing the number of store
rejections greatly. This means that 90% of the IPL products are QC checked
whereas a normal supplier would get around 2% checked.

As a consequence, IPL is driving down their customer complaints dramat-
ically. Although the standards are a lot tougher, for the whole business it
makes sense to have the onsite presence. Therefore QC at IPL is an integral
part of their vertically integrated supply chain.

Finally, fresh produce is a living product: the closer to store you can pick
and pack it, the better it is.

Daniel Angadi
Plant Operations Manager
IPL, part of the Wal-Mart Group

7.5 Suggestions for Further Reading

Hines, T. (2004). *Supply chain strategies: Customer driven and customer focused.*
Oxford: Butterworth-Heinemann.

References

Chopra, S., & Meindl, P. (2010). *Supply chain management: strategy, planning and operation.* Upper Saddle River, NJ: Pearson Prentice Hall.

Christopher, M. (2005). *Logistics and supply chain management: Creating value-added networks.* Harlow: Financial Times Prentice Hall.

Johnson, G., Scholes, K., & Whittington, R. (2008). *Exploring corporate strategy: text & cases (8th ed.).* Harlow: Financial Times Prentice Hall.

Johnson, G., Scholes, K., et al. (2008). *Exploring corporate strategy: Text and cases.* Harlow: Financial Times Prentice Hall.

Porter, M. E. (2004). *Competitive advantage: Creating and sustaining superior performance.* New York: Free Press.

Treacy, M., & Wiersema, F. (1997). *The discipline of market leaders: Choose your customers, narrow your focus, dominate your market.* New York: Basic Books.

Chapter 8
Guide to People in Supply Chain Management

Abstract This chapter guides you through people working within supply chain management, and it focuses on the learning and development element of people management. There are three parts of this chapter. First, we will look at learning and development from an organisational point of view and how to construct a learning and development strategy. Second, we will explore the value of leadership in a supply chain company and explain how effective leadership styles can be employed. Third, we consider how to improve learning by incorporating different learning styles in learning and development programmes with the ultimate goal to improve business performance. The chapter concludes with a case study of best practice on learning and development in the Unilever Supply Chain Academy.

Having read this chapter you will be able to:

- Clarify the tools to enable learning in a supply chain business
- Identify the value of leadership development in the supply chain world
- Explore how supply chain managers can better support individuals to learn and apply supply chain management concepts

8.1 The Importance of People in Supply Chain Organisations

It is the people who drive, innovate, challenge and improve supply chain operations. Therefore, an entire chapter will be dedicated to people within supply chain organisations. When we talk about people in supply chain, at least three perspectives come into mind:

1. Organisational
2. Team
3. Individual

In this chapter, we will focus on Learning and Development (L&D) aspects of all three perspectives. We will start with the organisational perspective looking at L&D strategy in an organisation. Next, we will look at the team perspective discussing team situations and leadership styles. Finally, we explore the individual perspective of learning in a supply chain context.

C. Scott et al., *Guide to Supply Chain Management*,
DOI 10.1007/978-3-642-17676-0_8, © Springer-Verlag Berlin Heidelberg 2011

8.1.1 Constructing a Learning and Development Strategy

We will first consider organisational learning and the L&D learning strategy in supply chain companies. Depending on a person's job role, a different set of supply chain skills and knowledge applies. Therefore different levels of learning will be required (see Fig. 8.1).

The pyramid to the left shows the different organisational levels. The pyramid to the right indicates different levels of learning according to Bloom's taxonomy (Forehand 2005). Let's have a look at each level of the learning strategy:

- Level 1: The first level forms the basis of supply chain learning that should be made available for the broader supply chain community. At this level, knowledge and understanding of basic SC concepts, processes, systems and roles are required. The pyramid is broadest here, which means that many people in your organisation should get wide access to the foundation level of supply chain practices. One example would be an e-learning course for your customer service personnel who need to know and understand the customer order lead-times, product portfolio and delivery options.
- Level 2: The second stage targets the operational level of different supply chain functions. Here, the employees of your company should be exposed to the application and analysis of supply chain principles necessary for their respective functions. This could be, for example, a one day training course for Stock Controllers who learn to compare stock figures with other warehouse locations and suggest improvement measures for safety, cycle and dead stock.
- Level 3: The last level targets managerial skills. At this level, the L&D agenda should incorporate courses and initiatives around the synthesis and

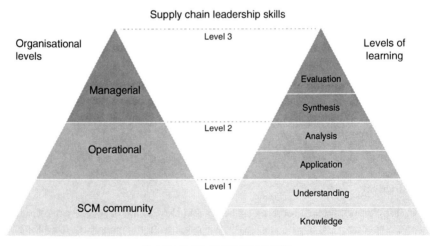

Fig. 8.1 Building a learning and development strategy

evaluation of supply chain issues. For example, a Planning Manager could be coached on the job on how to identify relevant KPIs for the planning team and how to link them to business targets and performance review.

In summary, on a continuum from business skills to leadership skills, each of these three organisational levels require a specific set of SC learning initiatives and courses that focus on different levels of learning. It is important that your company's SC professionals are equipped with the right skills and functional knowledge basis that they need for doing their job. An appropriate L&D strategy will help you to achieve this and maximise your team's performance. This should be underpinned with an appropriate and effective reward structure.

8.1.2 Linking Learning and Development to Supply Chain Strategies

The L&D strategy at all three levels should be closely linked to your overall supply chain strategy, outlined in Chap. 7 on Strategy. In order to make sure that the supply chain strategy is cascaded down, each employee's personal development plan should be linked in two steps (see Fig. 8.2).

To illustrate this concept, let's imagine that you work for a health care company that manufactures medical equipment for the Asian market. Part of your SC strategy could be to achieve these three strategic objectives:

1. *Superior service* to your South East Asian clients
2. *Constant cash flow* to invest in new innovations
3. *High stock turns* to minimise the cost of obsolescence

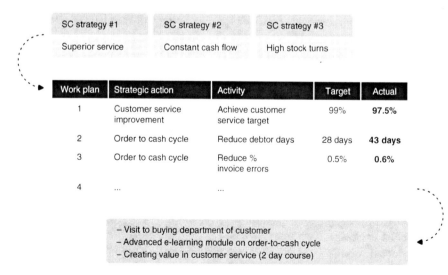

Fig. 8.2 Linking supply chain and personal development plan

In order to achieve these strategic objectives and to deliver high business performance, every director, manager, team leader and operator in your company should have a work plan that reflects strategic actions and activities that support the overall supply chain goals. In the example shown in Fig. 8.2, one of the work plan activities of a Customer Order Manager could be to reduce the debtor days from currently 43 days to 28 days (target). Thus, linking each work plan to the SC strategy is the first step in the process.

The second step is to find appropriate tools and initiatives to support achieving the work plan objectives. In the given example, the Customer Order Manager may be very experienced in customer service aspects of the role, but less so in the order-to-cash cycle management. Consequently, three activities as part of the Customer Order Manager's personal development plan could be agreed:

- Visit the customer buying department on a regular basis
- Complete advanced e-learning module on order-to-cash cycle
- Sign up for a customer service 2-day course

This example shows how the overall supply chain strategy should drive both work as well as personal development plan activities.

8.1.3 Encouraging a Learning Culture

We have talked about developing a learning and development concept and integrating it with your overall supply chain strategy and vision. A third area of learning strategy in supply chain companies is to establish a learning culture. In this context, the term learning organisation comes up in organisational literature, and it can be defined as an organisation that facilities learning among all members (Pedler et al. 1996).

Pedler et al. (1996) believe that the learning organisation is not achieved by simply training individuals, but that it can only happen as a result of every day learning at the organisational level. The authors take a wide view on defining the members of the learning organisation by describing them as employers, owners, customers, suppliers, and even competitors in some cases.

Characteristics of the learning organisation include a list of eleven development areas according to the authors (Pedler et al. 1996):

1. The learning approach to strategy
2. Participative policy making
3. Informating
4. Formative accounting and control
5. Internal exchange
6. Reward flexibility
7. Enabling structures
8. Boundary workers as environmental scanners

9. Inter-company learning
10. Learning climate
11. Self-development opportunities for all

The term *informating* refers back to the book "In the Age of the Smart Machine" by Shoshana Zuboff (1988). It describes the process that translates descriptions and measurements of activities, events and objects into information. In organisational learning, informating is the process of making information visible and accessible, e.g. through setting up an Intranet or shared drive. By doing so, these activities become meaningful to the organisation.

All of these eleven areas can be applied to learning in the supply chain context. Let's take, for example, the second point *participative policy making*. In a factory environment, new health and safety policies are introduced after an accident. Operators from different shifts are invited to a round table discussion on how the accident could have been prevented. Together, new safety measures are agreed and the new policy is introduced at the shop floor level. A variation of this approach could be using case studies of best practice that are developed and presented by factory teams. These examples of best practice show how a difficult task has been solved successfully and could lead to a company wide policy implementation. This participative approach may be much more effective than using a top-down approach that prevails in many factory environments.

An example of *reward flexibility* can be found in the reward and recognition process of, for example, the order management team. Here, cost can be saved if invoices are produced error-free. Therefore, rewards should be given to individuals if they achieve their performance target of no invoice error.

The decree to have *self-development opportunities for all* can be translated as follows: All supply chain employees should have access to a broad range of learning resources, like courses, workshops, seminars, self-learning material etc. In addition, they should be able to take part in one-to-one coaching with their line manager or an external coach and peer-to-peer information and best practice exchange. Development opportunities should also be part of bi-annual progress meetings between the employee and their supply chain manager to formalise the process.

Thus, following the approach of Pedler et al. (1996) the organisational L&D strategy should be supported by a general climate of organisational learning in order to maximise performance in your supply chain organisation.

8.2 Team Development in Supply Chain Management

This section will deal with a small – but important – element of team development and leadership literature, i.e. the adaptation of leadership styles and behaviour depending on the situation and the readiness of the employee, better known as situational leadership®.

We will first define leadership, introducing two dimensions of leadership behaviour. In the next step, we will identify different leadership situations and their corresponding leadership behaviour needs. Finally, we will apply a model of situation leadership and conclude with three abilities that a supply chain manager needs to acquire and practice in order to maximise team performance.

8.2.1 Dimensions of Situational Leadership®

The difference between management and leadership is often quoted as follows: Managers do things right whereas leaders are doing the right things. In fact, leadership in supply chain businesses is more than controlling, planning and administering the plan, source, make, deliver and return functions of goods in the supply chain. Leadership goes beyond that in creating a long-term vision, innovating and challenging existing processes, and above all inspiring people in the supply chain to maximise their performance.

For some supply chain managers, leadership behaviour comes naturally though they may not always be aware of the leadership style they use. For others, learning leadership behaviour is hard work that can involve a considerable amount of time until successfully applied. How you behave over time when you are trying to influence the performance of others is an area that has been studied thoroughly. There are two dimensions of behaviour in supply chain leadership:

1. Task orientation
2. People orientation

Task orientation is defined as the extent to which you engage in one-way communication; spell out the person's task; tell the person what to do, where to do it, and how to do it; and then oversee performance (Blanchard 2008). This leadership behaviour resembles at an extreme an autocratic style of leadership.

People orientation is the extent to which you engage in two-way communication, listen, provide support and encouragement, facilitate interaction and involve people in decision-making (Blanchard 2008). This leadership behaviour relates more to the people who are performing the task.

From these two basic dimensions, many leadership theories have been developed and written about leadership literature. The more widely known ones are the Managerial Grid (Blake and Mouton 1964) and the situational leadership® model (Hersey and Blanchard 1977). The rest of this section will focus on Hersey and Blanchard's (1977) situational leadership® model (see Fig. 8.3).

According to this model, there are four different leadership styles. The different leadership styles can be derived from different high-low combinations of the two dimensions just described. The different leadership styles are named, S1, S2, S3 and S4 and can be defined as follows (see Fig. 8.4).

Note that each style can be used with different people or in different work situations. The choice of style depends on your employee's competence and commitment while performing the job.

Fig. 8.3 Situational leadership[K] model adapted from Hersey et al. (2008)

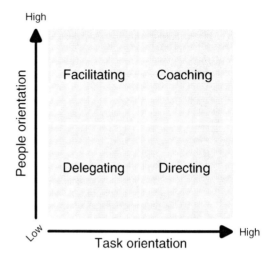

Fig. 8.4 Description of situational leadership[K] styles adapted from Hersey et al. (2008)

Style (S)		Description
S1	Directing	When you work with your team, you structure, organise, teach and supervise them.
S2	Coaching	You direct and support your team through coaching.
S3	Facilitating	Your main activities are to praise, listen and support.
S4	Delegating	In delegating, you turn over the responsibility for day-to-day decision making to your colleague.

8.2.2   Leadership and Team Development Levels

Let's imagine that you start a new job as a Warehouse Manager of a large building business. You are responsible for a small team of four people:

- Customer Service Manager
- Stock Controller
- Quality Manager
- Transport Manager

You have worked with the Customer Service Manager before in your old company and you know that she is very experienced and very competent. The stock controller, however, is fairly new in the role as he previously worked in the order picking team. Due to his high commitment and willingness to learn he recently got promoted to warehouse Stock Controller. Your Quality Manager has been in this role for the last eighteen years and is preparing for retirement next year. She performs her job on a routine basis and is not really committed to new projects – understandably as she is

Development level (D)	Description	Leadership style (S)
D1 – Unable but confident	People who lack competence but are enthusiastic and committed for work need direction and frequent feedback to get them started	S1 – Directing
D2 – Unable and insecure	For people who have some competence but are insecure and sometimes uncommitted to their job, the coaching leadership style works best. They need direction and feedback since they are at risk of not performing	S2 – Coaching
D3 – Able but insecure	Supporting leadership behaviour suits best people who are competent in their jobs but who lack confidence or work motivation.	S3 – Supporting
D4 – Able and confident	People who are both able and confident need very little supervision and support. For them the delegating style works best, as they are motivated and capable of steering day-to-day decision making without much intervention.	S4 – Delegating

Fig. 8.5 Development levels and leadership styles adapted from Hersey et al. (2008)

close to retirement. And lastly, your Transport Manager used to run the whole warehouse as an interim manager but decided after a year that the workload was too high and that a Warehouse Manager needed to be recruited. The Transport Manager enjoys working in his job and likes to share his knowledge with others.

The above situation describes four different employees with different levels of competence and commitment. Each of the four colleagues could thus be on a different development level. In a more recent version of the situational leadership® model, development levels are also called levels of performance readiness, and they are described as the extent to which a person in your team demonstrates the ability and willingness to accomplish a task (Hersey and Blanchard 1977). According to the authors, each of the leadership styles matches one of these development levels (see Fig. 8.5).

Thus the choice of leadership style depends on the development level of the employee or team. As employees develop over time, so should your leadership style. The direction of development should travel from directing towards delegating, as with delegation only low levels of directive as well as supportive behaviour are needed.

8.2.3 Matching Development Level and Leadership Style

As a Warehouse Manager, how can you best lead your team? Would you adopt a more directive leadership behaviour? Or would you show a more supportive behaviour?

The answer depends on your individual team members. What is good for the one might not be the most effective leadership style for the other. Let's review your new team composition and their most appropriate leadership style (S) depending on their development level (D):

1. Customer Service Manager – D3 and S3
2. Stock Controller – D1 and S1
3. Quality Manager – D2 and S2
4. Transport Manager – D4 and S4

In fact, you would treat each individual team member differently. For your Customer Service Manager, you would adopt a supporting leadership style where you praise, listen and facilitate mostly, your new stock controller would probably welcome a directing style where you structure, organise, teach and supervise him in his new role. A coaching style could suit your Quality Manager best to both direct and support her in her last year in her role. Since your Transport Manager used to be responsible for the entire warehouse operations you can easily turn over your responsibilities for day-to-day decision-making to him while making use of a delegating style.

Therefore we can see that different leadership styles work best for different people and/or different situations. If you used only the directing style for all of your team colleagues, you are in danger of your Customer Service Manager and your Transport Manager losing their motivation and commitment to you and deciding to leave the team. Those two might feel that with the directing you give them very little space to show their ability and competence. Likewise, if you used a mainly supporting style, your new Stock Controller as well as your Quality Manager could feel that they lack clarity of direction. In both situations, your business performance would suffer.

To summarise, the key for you to maximise your team performance lies in your ability to master the following three skills of situational leadership[R]:

1. Flexibility – you are flexible and able to use four different leadership styles: directing, coaching, supporting and delegating.
2. Diagnosis – you are able to judge the commitment of the individual team members
3. Partnering – you engage in performance planning, on the job coaching and performance evaluation together with the individual team member

8.3 Individual Learning of Supply Chain Professionals

The individual learning experience of supply chain professionals can be very different in one and the same classroom, online or on-the-job learning experience. After a course in supply chain management, the authors of this book received varied feedback regarding the content and style of the course from the delegates (see Fig. 8.6).

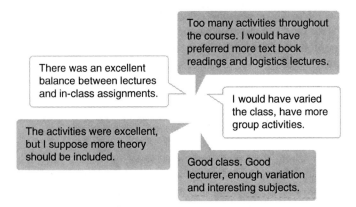

Fig. 8.6 Individual learning experience

What is the reason that some of the delegates rated it as a good course, whereas some others found either too little theory or too little activities during the two day intervention? One way of answering this question is to look at different learning styles and learning style preferences that we have found to play a role for effective training of supply chain professionals.

8.3.1 Four Types of Learning Styles

One of the most common and widely used classification of learning styles is the VARK model (Fleming 2001). This model is based on four personality dimensions: Visual, Auditory, Read/Write and Kinesthetic (VARK). The VARK model helps us to understand learning as it looks more closely at a particular aspect of employee perception and interaction with the learning materials. By applying VARK to business learning, we can increase the number of learning successes and improve our business through effective supply chain management learning.

According to the VARK model by Fleming (2001), there are four different learning styles that describe individual learning preferences, each linked to one of the senses and the way the brain works (see Fig. 8.7).

Visual preference learners acquire knowledge through seeing. These learners like to see the tutor's body language and facial expression, which helps them to fully understand the content of the session. Visual learners may think in pictures and symbols and learn best when key points are visually displayed. Flipchart diagrams, textbooks with illustrations, handouts and DVDs will support their learning process. Classroom learning sessions would be a preference for these learners.

Auditory preference learners acquire knowledge through listening. They learn best through verbal presentations, in-group discussions, talking things through and listening to others. Auditory learners take in and interpret the underlying meaning of speech by listening to the tone of voice, pitch and speed of the spoken word.

Learning style	These learners like to
Visual	See and imagine
Auditory	Listen and speak
Read/write	Read and write
Kinaesthetic	Touch and do

Fig. 8.7 VARK learning styles

They tend to remember better those things they have heard before even if that has never been documented in a written format. Auditory learners often benefit from reading out loud or recording voice. An e-learning course where a subject matter expert talks to the participant would be a preference for these learners.

Read/write preference learners acquire knowledge through working on text. These learners like to read through case studies, textbooks and other information sources in order to be able to contribute to the learning session. To provide an answer to a question asked in the classroom, read/write-preference learners enjoy drafting an outline of their answer before verbally stating it. During a speech or group discussion, these learners often prefer to take notes in order to absorb the information. A textbook with remotely coached assignment questions would be a preference for these learners.

Kinaesthetic preference learners acquire knowledge through moving and doing. These learners may find it hard to sit still for a longer period of time. They therefore learn best using a hands-on approach. Interactive learners like to actively explore the physical world around them. In-class simulations, practical challenges and activity-based group work suit best kinesthetic learners.

8.3.2 Learning in Supply Chain Management: Applying Different Styles

In supply chain learning, lectured facts sometimes dominate courses, such as figures, transportation modes, statistical forecast models and customer service KPI definitions. Factual information seems rather difficult to take in and digest depending on your learning style. Let's see how we can effectively apply style preferences to supply chain learning.

8.3.2.1 Understanding Complex Supply Chains: Have a Look

When we want to bring across the complexity of supply chains, it is not very effective just talking about it. Instead, we need to visualise the complexity of product and information flows, from the suppliers all the way through various retail channels to our customers. Therefore, we ask learners to engage in some simple supply chain mapping, and the effect is impressive. Visual learners suddenly recognise the geographic challenges of global supply chains identify the knock-on effect of transport delays and understand the relevance of efficient consumer response. When they come back to the workplace, they are able to depict their organisation's supply chain and work on real business improvements.

8.3.2.2 Improving Financial Performance Through Supply Chain Management: Listen Carefully

Translating supply chain performance into financial returns for you and your customer can be difficult. Yet, it is crucially important to understand how logistics activities impact business finance and strategy. We therefore like to invite guest speakers who talk about their experience in this field. How can asset utilisation be increased in order to make best use of capital invested? And how can you – as a Third Party Logistics provider – maximise your customer's Return on Capital Employed (ROCE)? For auditory learners, such sessions prove to be of great value. The spoken words of a Chief Financial Officer (CFO) can illuminate concepts that had not been understood before.

8.3.2.3 Benchmark Yourself and Learn from Best Practice: Read This

In order to bring industry examples of good supply chain practices into the classroom we often ask employees to do some pre- or overnight reading and to prepare some feedback. Business case studies that we seek from sources like the Harvard Business School do an excellent job. Especially learners with a read/write preference enjoy this part of supply chain learning. We give them time to read through and digest the written information individually. This way, they can internalise facts, learn about their industry and develop their own view on the cases described. By preparing some simple feedback, e.g. the ten main arguments, the learner is prepared to engage in classroom or smaller study group discussions. After returning to their workplace, these examples of best practice will be part of their vivid memory, and the employees will be able to benchmark their own business operations and strategies against those best practices.

8.3.2.4 Feeling the Pulse of the Supply Chain: Simulate It

Lastly, if you want to give hands-on experience of supply chain dynamics and stresses, use the "beer game" or other business simulations. These supply chain simulations reveal great learning on information and product flows, inventory management, the interaction of players in a product supply chain and the dynamics of amplified demand also known as the bullwhip effect. Kinaesthetic learners especially appreciate moving around and doing things. They show great learning performance in this element of supply chain learning. They are therefore more likely to internalise what's it like to be the wholesaler: stuck in the middle, with both supply and demand uncertainties. Also, they will physically feel the need to communicate and to share information about product supply and customer order. Back in their workplace, they can directly implement the value of information sharing and supply chain visibility.

8.3.3   Improving Performance Through Supply Chain Learning

Performance improvements should be the non-negotiable aim of all organisational learning initiatives. This is especially true for learning in supply chain management, where we still find a lot of untapped potential.

Whether training-on-the job, e-learning or classroom training, we need to acknowledge the difference in learning styles among employees. Employees who are stimulated to use their preferred style while learning will be engaging more during the course, and they will be motivated to successfully conclude the programme. Moreover, these employees will be able to transform the learning into vital actions for business improvement.

Putting learning style theory into supply chain learning practice will enable us to remember both tacit concepts as well as implicit consequences even a few weeks after the training course. This way we will come back with clear actions on process improvements ensuring long-term supply chain learning for your organisation.

8.4   Case Study of Best Practice in People: Supply Chain Academy

Accenture and Unilever partner up to build comprehensive learning framework and platform

When Unilever's Supply Chain Academy (hereafter abbreviated as the Academy) was first established together with Accenture in its current form in early 2006, the company set out to define a vision and mission that continues to guide us. The vision was built around three legs:

1. Business partnering whereby the Academy worked alongside the functional leadership teams identify learning needs
2. People capability solutions in which the Academy built partnerships with key providers to deliver what was required;

(continued)

3. Space for sharing where Unilever leverage their portal platform to deliver learning and other capability tools direct to customers' laptops

The mission sums Unilever's approach as "building people capabilities to deliver the supply chain strategy". Simplifying this, the company's guiding statement is best summarised as, "we don't allow people to fail because they haven't got access to the learning or tools they need to perform in their roles." In designing a new approach to supply chain learning in Unilever, the Academy team has developed a series of learning frameworks covering each of the supply chain sub processes as identified in the SCOR model.

Learning framework

Unilever's most recent work focuses on procurement (Source) and brings together many of the elements identified in this chapter. In designing a new framework for procurement learning, the company first set out to design a framework for procurement within Unilever, against which we could align learning.

The mechanics of the learning needs analysis have included:

- Internal scans including assessments against defined procurement skills, procurement strategy and stakeholder interviews
- External scans including literature reviews and insights from leaders in the field of procurement both academic and practicing

These inputs then allowed the development of a framework against which to "hang" learning, split between the strategic/leadership area and that of operations, which covers areas such as supplier management and risks in procurement. A learner can click on any part of the framework to open up a mapping of the available learning.

Existing learning has been assessed for its relevance and then mapped to the appropriate area on the framework. Mapping splits learning into general skills, professional skills and those interventions leading to a formal qualification in the area. The business also identified relevant articles from across the external bodies to which Unilever subscribes as well as providing links to appropriate sites for further research. All learning interventions are identified as e-learning, classroom based or other and a key approach for us has also been to identify and develop relations with globally relevant accrediting institutes.

Course development

As part of the company's work in procurement, Unilever developed two new classroom courses for managers and directors. Both of these courses fully align with the procurement framework using this to identify the key themes and modules of the course as well as the split between strategic input and operational focus. In the management course the split is 30% strategic

(continued)

and 70% operational with a move to half the content becoming strategic focused in the director level course.

The management level course starts on Monday midday, specifically to allow participants to fly that day rather than Sunday night and finishes mid afternoon on a Friday. Each day of the course has a theme be it strategic or operational and as well as providing input from Unilever speakers, a single course faculty provides the theoretical background and examples at each stage. The business provides a presentation from a supplier or customer to gain a different perspective and a whole day based on a procurement simulation to allow experiential learning of the concepts discussed and examples given. The course finishes with input from a member of the Unilever Procurement Leadership Team sharing their personal leadership journey and view of the challenges ahead. The approach seems to be the right one, with the initial pilot scoring 4.7 out of 5.

Next steps

Unilever's next steps are to map all learning to standard job descriptions and job skills profiles that we are developing for the new procurement organisation. The company will also launch a revised procurement careers framework making clear links back into supply chain and general management roles.

Through the learning framework approach learners can easily identify the best learning for themselves and their team members. The Academy also helps Unilever's employees to identify the necessary development steps for their future roles.

Rachel Thomas

Unilever

Director of Global Learning and Supply Chain Academy

8.5 Suggestions for Further Reading

Blanchard, K., Zigarmi, P., Zigarmi, D. (2004). *Leadership and the One Minute Manager*. London: Harper Collins Publisher

References

Blake, R. R., & Mouton, J. S. (1964). *The managerial grid*. Houston, TX: Gulf.

Blanchard, K. (2008). Situational leadership: Adapt your style to suit their development level. *Leadership Excellence, 25*(5), 19.

Fleming, N. (2001). *Teaching and learning styles: VARK strategies*. New Zealand: Christchurch.

Forehand, M. (2005). Bloom's taxonomy: Original and revised. In M. Orey (Ed.), Emerging perspectives on learning, teaching, and technology, Athens (GA): University of Georgia.

Hersey, P., & Blanchard, K. H. (1977). *Management of organizational behavior: Utilizing human resources.* Englewood Cliffs, NJ: Prentice-Hall.

Hersey, P., Blanchard, K., & Johnson, D. (2008). *Management of organizational behavior: Leading human resources.* Upper Saddle River, NJ: Pearson Education.

Pedler, M., Burgoyne, J. G., & Boydell, T. (1996). *The learning company: a strategy for sustainable development.* New York: McGraw-Hill.

Zuboff, S. (1988). *In the age of the smart machine.* New York: Basic Books.

Chapter 9
Guide to Finance in Supply Chain Management

Abstract This chapter guides you through the topic of finance in supply chain management. First, it clarifies why supply chain companies are in business. Second, it explores what impacts supply chain management has on the key financial statements of an organisation, in particular the profit and loss, balance sheet and cash flow statements. Third, it highlights how the supply chain can add value and improve corporate financial performance, by looking at its influence over return on capital employed. The chapter concludes with a case study of best practice at the company NWF, who provide supply chain services to improve return on capital employed for their customers.

Having read this chapter you will be able to:

- Clarify why supply chain companies are in business
- Recognise the impact of supply chain management on the key financial statements
- Demonstrate how supply chain management can add value and improve corporate financial performance

9.1 Introduction to Supply Chain Finance

9.1.1 The Business Process

Supply chain companies are usually in business to generate cash and give a return to their investors. Also making a profit is important, we can calculate profit by taking our costs for the year and deduct it from the sales for the year. However, whilst companies are still able to continue operating when making no profit or having losses for several years, they immediately stop operating when they run out of cash. The authors recommend an excellent text on this subject written by Tennent (2008), which guides people though the main financial principles, illustrates their application and finally provides a toolkit for managing financial responsibility. In order to understand the different financial parameters of a company, the business process can be illustrated (see Fig. 9.1).

C. Scott et al., *Guide to Supply Chain Management*,
DOI 10.1007/978-3-642-17676-0_9, © Springer-Verlag Berlin Heidelberg 2011

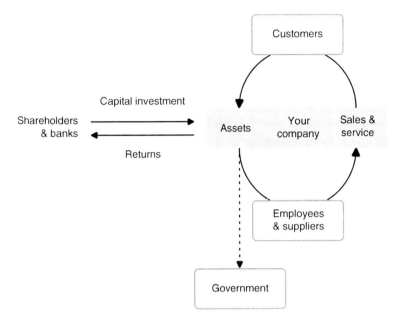

Fig. 9.1 The business process

Let's consider an example and assume you would like to start a new company that manufactures drinks, similar to Schweppes or the Coca-Cola Company. You would need some initial *capital investment* in order to buy *assets*. Assets are, for example, the factory, raw materials or perhaps trucks to deliver the finished products. The *shareholders and banks* on the left, which can be considered as the two sources of *capital investment*, provide their investment in the form of cash. This is represented by the arrow from shareholders and banks to assets in the centre of the diagram.

Once the assets have been purchased, *your company* can start selling the drinks product. In order to do so, *employees and suppliers* must be paid for their work, products and services. The arrow from assets to *sales and service* represents cash flow out of the business as the employees and suppliers are paid. The drinks products are then sold to *customers*, who pay the business. This is depicted by the top right arrow as cash received from customers. If the business sells the drinks for more than the costs involved with manufacture and distribution, a profit is made. This profit is then subject to tax paid to the *government*. Finally, from the cash remaining, *returns* are paid back to the shareholders and banks through interest and dividends as indicated by the arrow on the bottom left. Any monies left over can be retained and reinvested in the business to generate, for example, growth. Now let us consider three areas critical to supply chain finance: gearing, returns and hurdle rates.

9.1.2 Gearing

The term gearing in business finance identifies how much capital investment in the company is funded by internal or external funds. It is the measure of financial leverage, demonstrating the degree to which a firm's activities are funded by owner's funds, e.g. shareholders, versus creditor's funds, e.g. banks. Capital that is lent by banks is referred to as debt and capital that is invested by the shareholders is referred to as equity. Gearing is a measure and is expressed as:

Gearing = Debt as a percentage of total funds (debt + equity).

In many businesses, 30–50% of debt is seen as an ideal range of gearing. Managers often ask why businesses are not solely financed by bank debt alone. To answer this question, we need to think about risk. Banks feel reluctant to take 100% of the risk alone and therefore prefer to engage in capital investments where a substantial part is given by shareholders.

9.1.3 Returns

Let's return to our drinks company example. In order to start a drinks company, the banks will inject some investment (say 50%), and the remaining capital will have to be obtained from investors (shareholders). Both these parties will require a return from the drinks business. For example, the banks would expect a 5% return in interest and shareholders a 10% return – this seems less favourable for the banks. If the drinks company goes bankrupt, the banks own the assets and the shareholders lose everything. By taking more risk the shareholders can receive higher dividends (annual payments) and capital growth of the shares they have in the business.

9.1.4 Hurdle Rates

As you already know, the return rates have two main components: the cost of debt capital and cost of equity capital. This is referred to as the Cost Of Capital (COC). Most companies are financed by a combination of debt and equity so they need to find a balanced combination of these two. For example, 50% of the company might be financed by debt and 50% by equity. If debt requires a 5% and equity a 15% return then the Weighted Average Cost of Capital (WACC) is 10%. This 10% WACC is known as the "hurdle rate". The hurdle rate can be described as the required return for a project. A company planning to invest in a new factory, for example, needs to make sure that the return of the investment is greater than the WACC before the investment starts paying off financially. Supply chain projects need to satisfy at least the returns to the lenders, or there is no benefit to the business and no financial reason why the project should take place.

Managers who work in third party logistics companies have the even harder task of jumping two hurdles. Not only do their solutions need to yield greater returns than their customers' hurdle rate, they also need to satisfy their own company hurdle rates before they can go ahead and implement any solution.

9.2 How Companies Cascade Financial Information

Companies cascade financial information using three financial statements: profit and loss account, balance sheet and cash flow statement (Stickney et al. 2009). The profit and loss account is a detailed summary of the sales revenue for one financial year and the associated costs. The balance sheet summarises how the company has been financed. The cash flow statement shows the cash in and the cash out for the business, in a given year. Remember from the business process covered earlier that the four arrows represent cash.

9.2.1 Profit and Loss

The Profit and Loss (P&L) account is sometimes referred to as the income statement, and it essentially captures how much money goes into and out of the company. It usually consists of four parts (see Fig. 9.2).

		€
	Revenue	X
Part 1	Cost of sales	(Y)
	Gross profit	Z
Part 2	Operating expenses	(Y)
	Operating profit	Z
	Interest	(Y)
Part 3	Tax	(Y)
	Profit after tax	Z
Part 4	Dividend	(Y)
	Retained profit	Z

Fig. 9.2 Profit and loss account

The first part is a trading account, showing the total sales *revenue* less the *costs of sales* and any changes in the value of stock from the last accounting period. This gives the *gross profit* (or loss). The second part shows any other income (apart from trading) and lists administrative and other costs to arrive at an *operating profit* (or loss). From this operating profit the appropriate corporation tax is deducted to give the third part, which is the net *profit after tax*. In the fourth part, *dividends* (returns to shareholders) are subtracted from profit after tax; this results in *retained profit*.

Supply chain activities can impact the P&L very significantly by influencing both revenue and cost. It is useful at this point to consider four criteria against which we can illustrate this influence:

- Quality
- Service
- Cost
- Time

Should manufacturing be substandard or the distribution processes not deliver the required *quality* of a product, sales will decrease. If we forecast inefficiently, it might result in a short delivery to a customer, so that the *service* level is affected. *Cost* can be considered from a competitive perspective rather than the absolute number. If two products are very similar, but one is more expensive than the other to produce because its supply chain is less efficient, sales revenue is likely to be less. In some of the companies in which the authors have worked, supply chain costs made up between 25 and 70% of total costs. Examples of supply chain costs are:

- Raw material purchases
- Salaries
- Factory conversion costs
- Depreciation on supply chain assets
- Facility energy costs
- Insurance and utilities for facilities
- Fuel for vessels and vehicles
- Inventory storage and interest
- Inventory write off/obsolescence

Higher profit margins will be achieved through reduced supply chain costs. It has therefore become a key objective of supply chain managers to reduce costs without reducing the three other criteria of quality, service and time.

The final criterion is the supply chain impact on *time*. Supply chains influence the time it takes to get a product to the market place. This could either be a customer ordering a product and waiting for a delivery or a new product launch. An example might be the electronics or telecommunications industry, where new innovations are core to success. For example, the initial launch of touch pad mobile phone functionality gave Apple a considerable first mover advantage in the marketplace until its competitors followed suit. The iPhone launch was successfully supported by short-lead times between R&D, manufacturing and retailers. Supply chains therefore can increase sales revenue by the speed at which they can move products to market or customers.

9.2.2 Balance Sheet

The balance sheet is the financial statement of a business that lists the assets, debts, and owners' investment as of a specific date, very much like a "snap-shot" in time. An example structure is depicted (see Fig. 9.3).

On the balance sheet, all items are owned by the company. Within *fixed assets*, *buildings* include factories and warehouses. *Plant and machinery* comprises vessels, trucks and heavy machinery used in manufacturing. An interesting decision point is whether to own or to lease facilities. Once buildings and equipment are leased, they disappear from the balance sheet and become costs that appear on the profit and loss account.

Moving onto *current assets*, *stock* refers to inventory in the format of raw material, work in progress or finished goods. *Debtors* are customers that still have not paid for their purchases. Interestingly, if the supply chain fails in its commitment to customers, they are less likely to pay on time. If this occurs, the debtor days might increase. When all orders are delivered in full, on time and with perfect quality, shorter credit can be negotiated with customers. Similarly, suppliers might be included in the balance sheet as they are people to whom the company owes money. A credit card company might ask us to pay our debts in 30 days; hence the credit card company is our creditor. In the same way, a supplier might ask its customer to pay its debts in 30 days. A customer could then be able to negotiate better creditor days by virtue of its supply chain activity.

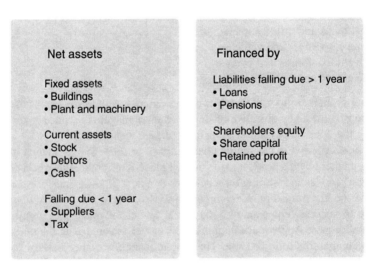

Fig. 9.3 A simple balance sheet

The remaining elements of the balance sheet are covered substantially in the finance literature and we suggest sources for further reading below. We shall concentrate here on the main supply chain influences.

9.2.3 Cash Flow

Business cash flow is more difficult to picture than profit. To clarify the concept of cash flow, it is often helpful to consider activities that would increase or decrease cash flow.

As discussed in the balance sheet section of this book, if physical assets are leased rather than owned, they appear in the P&L and no longer the balance sheet. The decision to lease rather than to own the asset would also improve cash flow. An example would be a customer, who wanted to buy a car from a dealer for €10,000. If the customer had €10,000 in cash and not a single cent more, they could buy the car but would have a poor cash flow. To resolve this cash flow issue, they could lease the car rather than buy it. In this case, the car would not count as an asset, but appear on the P&L under lease costs.

If customers pay sooner and suppliers are paid later, both of these strategies improve cash flow. For example, if a company tells its employees that payroll would like to pay them at the beginning of the month rather than wait until the end, there would be few complaints. Likewise, if a credit card company, who normally requires payment within 30 days, kindly tells its customers they can pay within 90 days, few customers will complain.

Reducing inventory is also a way the supply chain can improve cash flow in a business. This is a key issue for companies who hold stock. Retailers such as Wal-Mart, Carrefour or Tesco would all like to reduce inventory to improve their cash flow. Rather than tie up cash in inventory, they would most likely want to invest that cash in new store openings. If they have too much inventory and still want to open new stores, then they would have to seek more capital investment from shareholders or banks. Consequently, reducing inventory gives businesses cash without needing to raise extra capital.

As supply chains become increasingly global, companies are affected by exchange rate variance. An example is the Turkish sugar company who buys sugar from the US. It would sell the sugar product in Turkish Lira but would be buying in US dollars. If the Turkish Lira devalued against the US dollar, the Turkish company would be adversely affected. Companies can "hedge" against currency fluctuations by using their treasury departments to buy different currencies and hold these to buffer against fluctuations. However, companies can also use their supply chain to improve cash flow by switching manufacturing to countries with a weak exchange rate. For example, if Ford is manufacturing cars in the Euro zone and the British Pound becomes weaker than the Euro, they can move more manufacturing volume into Britain.

Interestingly, all three financial statements can be improved by managing inventory well. The costs would be reduced through less storage needs, the assets would be reduced through holding less inventory and possibly less warehouses, and finally the cash flow would improve.

9.3 How to Add Value and Improve Corporate Financial Performance

Organisations communicate financial information internally and externally, using the Return On Capital Employed (ROCE) formula (see Fig. 9.4).

ROCE, which is referred to as a percentage, can be calculated by taking the profit from the P&L and dividing it by the capital employed from the balance sheet as discussed previously. The larger the ROCE percentage figure becomes, the higher a return the investor will receive. It is likely that investors will monitor ROCE for different companies and base their investment decisions on the historical and forecasted ROCE performance (Atrill and McLaney 2006).

9.3.1 Supply Chain Impact on ROCE

The ROCE model can be expanded into a hierarchy of ratios (Vause 2009). This hierarchy of ratios can be useful for supply chain managers as they can map how their supply chain operations influence their overall financial performance (see Fig. 9.5).

Supply chain improvements can be quickly and easily linked to an increase or decrease in *ROCE*. For example, if *sales* are higher through improved delivery performance, then *profit* will increase. If *material* quality is improved, less materials and labour are wasted, therefore costs will decrease and profit will increase. When *labour* or *overheads* are efficiently utilised, this will also impact favourably against costs and profit.

If, through improved management, the number of *stocks* is reduced, this means fewer current assets and subsequently a better use of capital employed. If the *debtor*

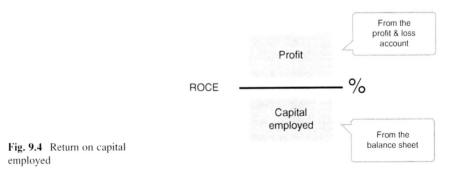

Fig. 9.4 Return on capital employed

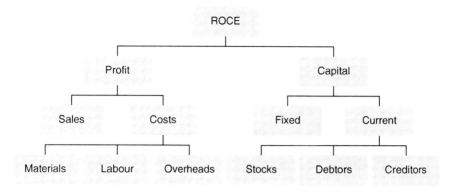

Fig. 9.5 A hierarchy of ratios

days are minimised and the *creditor* days maximised, this will improve the cash to cash cycle and reduce the amount of current assets required for the business. The company Zara, for example, operates on a negative working capital, which is a remarkable achievement in the retailing sector (ICMR 2006).

Through these actions, there are multiple impacts on ROCE as profit margins increase and capital is utilised more efficiently.

An example from three of the world's largest oil companies BP (A), Shell (B) and Exxon (C) can be seen in Fig. 9.6. The numbers are taken from their annual reports.

In the example year shown, both company A and B achieved a healthy ROCE of 30.8% and 29.3%. This means that if an investor put €1 into each of these two companies, then the return at the end of the year would be €0.308 and €0.293 respectively. However, if the investor had chosen to invest in Company C in this example, the investor would have returned 55.6% or €0.556 from a €1 investment. By improving ROCE the benefit is that investors are more likely to be attracted to invest in the business. Therefore, supply chain improvement initiatives should always have a positive influence on the company's ROCE.

9.3.2 Applying Six Supply Chain Performance Levers

It is important for supply chain managers to quickly focus on areas in the business that can influence financial performance positively. There are six factors that reoccur in companies with supply chains. They behave like levers, i.e. when pulled they improve supply chain financial performance (see Fig. 9.6).

The six supply chain performance levers can be used as a checklist when auditing supply chains (see Fig. 9.7). Used wisely, they can impact positively on the lower levels of the hierarchy of ratios. The six levers are shown in Fig. 9.7.

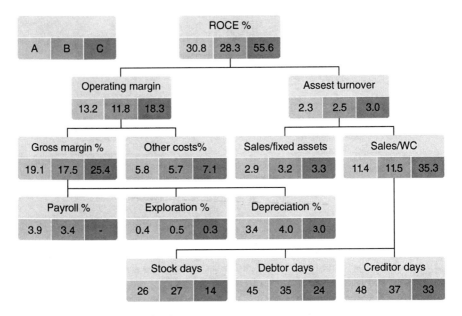

Fig. 9.6 Example hierarchy of ratios

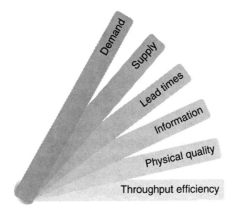

Fig. 9.7 Six supply chain performance levers

If we take the "river" analogy explored earlier in Chap. 2 on Plan, you can construct the six levers listed above.

At each downstream element of the supply chain, the customer transfers *demand* onto the next stage up in the chain. This demand can be in the form of a forecast or order, and this is where the supply chain starts. We therefore call this our first lever.

Conversely, upstream from each element we have the *supply* of product. The on time in full delivery performance of product supply is imperative in the overall effectiveness of the chain. Without supply we cannot satisfy demand. So this is our second lever.

As we have seen in the examples above, the *lead-time* and responsiveness is a key measure of success within the chain. Do we have an extended factory to customer lead-time where product is being delivered around the world or do we have a quick response chain that responds quickly to demand volatilities? Lead-time is our third supply chain performance leaver.

The fourth and fifth levers relate to the two main flows within the supply chain that were outlined in the introduction chapter – namely product and information flow. *Information* is important to advise the delivery time and to ensure the correct product is shipped to the correct place. Products should arrive at the customer's in good shape without any defects or damage. Therefore, *physical quality* needs to be recorded.

Finally, *throughput efficiency* has been chosen as the last lever of supply chain performance. This refers to the amount of working capital in the chain and the efficiency of the network. It is the proportion of valued activities over non-valued added activities.

In Fig. 9.8, we can see the impact of improving demand capture on ROCE.

Let's say that 180 units of product are forecasted by a manufacturer and subsequently produced. However, the actual demand comes in for 200 products and the manufacturer can only deliver what is made. Thus, the customer is short delivered by 20 and the manufacturer has a lost sales opportunity. If the demand forecasting is improved and the manufacturer achieves an improved forecast of 200, the sales revenue will be increased. In this example we can improve ROCE three times. First, we are likely to sell more because we correctly forecasted and captured demand. Since we have less demand uncertainty, we don't need to hold as much safety stock. This is the second improvement that will positively influence ROCE. Thirdly, as we are holding less stock, we don't need as much warehouse space. Thus, by improving forecast accuracy we might even be able to reduce our fixed assets.

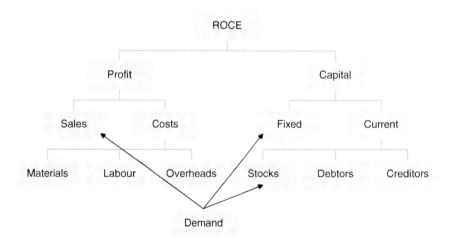

Fig. 9.8 Demand impact on the hierarchy of ratios

The other five supply chain performance levers work in a similar way. Improved supply means the supply chain carries out activities on time. By reducing lead-times inventory is lowered, safety stocks are less and forecasting is more accurate. Better information flows reduce raw material waste, wasted labour and overheads. Optimising this area could also lead to lower stocks, faster payment and improved working capital. Better physical quality positively impact materials, labour, overheads, stocks and potentially debtors and creditors. Finally, improved throughput efficiency means that product is pulled through the supply chain with less waste and less waiting time.

9.4 Case Study of Best Practice in Finance: NWF

Improving return on capital employed for NWF customers
This case study is focused on the NWF Group PLC's food distribution business unit that is called Boughey Distribution. Boughey Distribution consists primarily of the customer's distribution of ambient grocery products that require storage and shared delivery to major supermarket regional distribution centres. This case study shows how Boughey Distribution could improve ROCE for its customers.
Background
Food manufacturers and importers delivering to the major supermarket groups face challenging distribution problems, particularly if they don't have the volume for full load deliveries. Some of the problems are:

- Owning distribution assets (trucks and warehouses)
- Poor productivity in distribution (inefficient truck load fill)
- Having the competences in the business to manage competitive distribution

Food manufacturers need cash to invest in new products or plants to grow and remain competitive. They don't want to put this valuable resource into warehouses and truck assets. Also without consistent high volumes, truckload fill is not optimised giving a high cost for each pallet delivery.

Strategically, food manufacturers and importers may see running their own warehousing and road transport as non-core and a large distraction for their management teams. This lack of expertise may also affect sales and/or quality negatively compared to the competition. In addition, inefficiencies in distribution lead to companies holding more stock than they need to, drawing in yet more cash from the business. From a financial perspective, all these problems reduce ROCE for food manufacturers and importers.

(continued)

Making a change

To change the traditional set-up in the industry, food manufacturers and importers (customers) can outsource their distribution to Boughey. Let's consider the three problems mentioned above.

Firstly, if customers want to distribute their products to the major supermarket group's distribution centres, they need distribution assets, which in the main are trucks and warehouses. If these are purchased outright, then customers will invest their own cash in these assets. This removes cash from their business, restricting them from doing the things they would like to do and also reducing ROCE. However, by outsourcing to Boughey they no longer require the assets, releasing cash and improving their ROCE.

Secondly, customers with less than a full truckload run the risk of poor productivity. One solution is to make and hold more stock and incentivise the retailer to buy full loads to maximise load fill. This will both reduce margin and increases the inventory cost for the business. Another solution is consolidation, bringing together and mixing pallets from different customers. For example, if the optimum pallet capacity of a truck is twenty-six pallets, then any load lower than this figure will immediately cause an increase cost per pallet that the customer needs to pay for. This is because the fixed and running costs of the truck are the same whether it has a full load or not. By consolidating pallets from different customers, who need to deliver to the same major supermarket group's distribution centre, Boughey is able to make up full loads. The cost per pallet therefore remains as low as possible and this saving can be passed onto the customers. As cost per pallet delivered by Boughey is lower than the customers could achieve on their own, the customers' ROCE has again been improved.

Finally, food manufacturers and importers are not necessarily experts in managing competitive distribution. By using the Boughey warehousing and transport network it is more likely that there is a positive impact on the customers' revenue and quality, than if they had been managing these themselves. Greater revenue and quality drives an improved margin and hence a positive impact on ROCE.

The challenge

The challenge is to be able to distribute full loads on a daily basis, retain and develop expertise while working with some of the largest blue chip food brands and retailers in the grocery sector. Achieving this requires sophisticated inventory control systems to ensure correct rotation of products and full traceability from point of receipt to delivery. In addition, goods need to be held on behalf of around 200 different customers.

A single site facility is needed that can carry out packing, labelling, shrink wrapping, flow wrapping, sleeving and bar coding plus inspection and promotional packing services. Also, there needs to be an information system in place that links Boughey's to their direct customers and their retail customers.

(continued)

Finally deliveries need to be made nationally by road to the full range of supermarket, wholesale and speciality chains.

Positive results

In summary, from a ROCE perspective, customers will see an improvement by outsourcing distribution to Boughey. This can be through increased sales, lower distribution costs, reduced assets and improved working capital. This will give Boughey's customers to reduce inventory and increase their on time delivery performance, which in turn brings them in a better situation to discuss improved creditor days with the major supermarkets.

John Ford

Finance Director

NWF PLC

9.5   Suggestions for Further Reading

Higson, C. J. (2006). *Financial statements: Economic analysis and interpretation.* London: Rivington.

Pratt, J. & Hirst, D. (2008). *Financial reporting for managers: A value-creation perspective.* Chichester: John Wiley & Sons.

References

Atrill, P., & McLaney, E. J. (2006). *Accounting and finance for non-specialists.* Harlow: Pearson Education Ltd.

ICMR. (2006). *Zara's supply chain management practices* (p. 13). Hyderabad: Centre for Management Research.

Stickney, C. P., Weil, R. L., Schipper, K., & Francis, J. (2009). *Financial accounting: An introduction to concepts, methods and uses.* Florence, KY: South-Western Publishing.

Tennent, J. (2008). *Guide to financial management (The Economist).* London: Bloomberg Press.

Vause, B. (2009). *Guide to analysing companies.* London: Profile Books Ltd.

Chapter 10
Guide to Customer Service in Supply Chain Management

Abstract The chapter guides you through the topic of customer service in supply chain management. This chapter is structured as follows: first, it explains what customer service is and who our supply chain customers are. Second, it explores how we can manage key customers' lifetime value and creating customer service ambassadors. Third, it explains how we can deliver against customer needs by working to agreed standards and the importance of service recovery. The chapter concludes with a best practice case study on winning in the marketplace through customer service in the company Unilever South Africa.

Having read this chapter you will be able to:

- Explain what customer service is and who our supply chain customers are
- Clarify how we can manage our key customers
- Explore how we can deliver against customer needs

10.1 Introduction to Customer Service

Customer service exists for a reason: improved business performance. It can also become a real differentiator and key component of competitive advantage for a supply chain business. The benefits of this can be summarised using the service profit chain model (Heskett and Sasser 2010:120) (see Fig. 10.1).

The service profit chain demonstrates the fundamental link between business performance and customer service. It starts by stating that *internal service quality*, which is about treating internal customers with a high level of service, drives *employee satisfaction*. This is because employees like to be treated with the core customer values of respect and dignity. This satisfaction then drives *employee loyalty* and *productivity* as staff stays longer in companies they are satisfied with and work more efficiently. From this, the employees then provide a greater level of *external service value*, which drives a higher level of external *customer satisfaction*. *Customer loyalty* is built from higher satisfaction and finally, with a loyal customer base, companies can achieve greater *revenue growth* and *profitability*.

C. Scott et al., *Guide to Supply Chain Management*,   155
DOI 10.1007/978-3-642-17676-0_10, © Springer-Verlag Berlin Heidelberg 2011

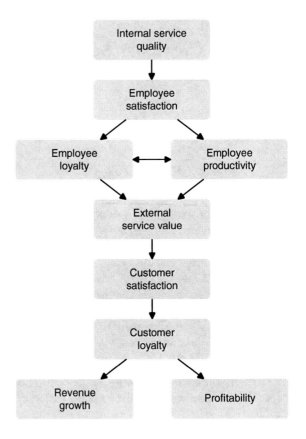

Customer service is an emotional topic that can bring out strong passionate views from people. Most of us have stories we can tell about great service we have received, where a company has "gone the extra mile" to improve our customer experience. This could be from a hotel, restaurant, airline or call centre to give a few examples. Unfortunately, we also have long-lasting memories of terrible service we have received! We tell people these experiences and share the good and bad news.

It is our ability to provide a consistently good service rather than a mixed variety of excellent and poor service that helps customers to build perceptions about us and therefore helps them decide whether they will buy from us or not. There are many different definitions of customer service written but a concise summary for today's supply chain organisations might be:

> Customer service is the ability of an organisation to constantly and consistently exceed the customer's needs and expectations (Emmet 2007: 14).

From a supply chain perspective if a company has similar quality, costs and lead-times as its competitors, then a key area of competitive advantage is the customer service it offers. This chapter addresses customer service from a supply chain

Business-to-Business (B2B) point of view, as apposed to the Business-to-Customer/
Consumer (B2C). In supply chain companies this external B2C customer service
activity perhaps only takes place at the last point downstream. Importantly and often
overlooked, there will be a high level of internal customer service activity taking
place, where employees provide a service for other employees within the same
organisation. The same service experience emotions can be triggered upstream in
the supply chain within these B2B interactions.

10.1.1   Who Are Our Customers?

Companies with supply chains still have a great opportunity to tap into largely
uncharted customer service potential in their businesses. Let's first consider who
our customers are.

We can split customers into external and internal customers. Interestingly, when
an external customer asks for assistance, organisations tend to strive to help them
and make sure that the customer receives great service. However, when an
internal customer requires support, for example the sales department contacting
the warehouse to find out how much stock is available; it is not uncommon that
they are treated with a lower perceived level of service. This is unfortunate, as
we saw with the service profit chain earlier; the first step is to treat your
employees as internal customers, and only then external customer service can
be improved.

If you ask different internal functions within your organisation what service they
receive from their own colleagues, the results are sometimes quite shocking. This
can be even more concerning when we recall that our external customer service is
reflected ultimately by our internal customer service. To deliver great customer
service we should treat our internal customers as external customers. The hotel
group Ritz Carlton encompasses this through their credo: "We are ladies and
gentlemen serving ladies and gentlemen". In other words, in all dealings they
have internally, they have the same values when dealing with external customers.
This helps driving the service profit chain as explained earlier.

When companies outsource functions, for example distribution, the new distribution company is no longer an internal supplier. They simply have no choice but to
offer a better service or risk losing the business. An example here would be the
UK's largest brewer "Bass" (now Molson Coors) who outsourced its internal
distribution to DHL. The same employees worked for a different company and
had a "real" customer for the first time that dictated the service requirement agenda
rather than the other way round. This resulted in an improvement in service for the
whole company, demonstrating the power of treating internal employees as external
customers.

One good customer service exercise the authors have posed is to ask people who
their customers are. Some of the common answers are:

- The shopper
- The end user
- The consumer who uses the product
- The retailer who buys the product from the supplier

These are of course all very important customers. Let us further consider the question by studying the retail supply chain for a chocolate snack, from the suppliers to the consumers. In reality we can see that there are many more customers that have to be served (see Fig. 10.2).

Following the *downstream supply chain*, the *suppliers* deliver direct to the retailer customer's depot. The *retail depot* is in this case the primary customer point. As we move further downstream in the supply chain we encounter more customers. On arrival in the store, the *goods receipt* staff need to identify the product quickly and handle it carefully so it won't get damaged easily. The *retail back of store* personnel might have in excess of 20,000 other products to manage and need to be able to find the chocolate product quickly and easily. The shelf *replenishment* team want products that are easy to open from their outer cases (the corrugated cardboard box that contains chocolate snacks) and are even easier to stack. If our chocolate product does not fit these criteria, these customers will be less likely to put our product on the shelf with a risk of out of stock more often. The *shopper* is a key customer who needs to recognise our product and who decides to buy it. The *retail checkout* needs to find the barcode and scan it correctly. The product then moves to the end *consumers* who eat the chocolate bar. Undoubtedly, we would have missed some customers if we had not gone into this level of detail on our supply chain journey.

To achieve great service it is important to consider these different interactions, some of which are almost intangible but have a huge impact on the product reaching the consumer. Customers have high expectations and they will expect as a minimum that we will deliver the promise, which is sometimes referred to as the core service. But how do we understand what that promise is, given the intangible multiple interaction points along the supply chain?

10.1.2 Managing Variability to Improve Customer Service

Even with the best S&OP process (see Chap. 2 on Plan), the supply chain is consistently struggling to cope with dynamic changes in both demand and supply. Imagine a business that had smooth demand, notified with lots of lead-time, reliable supply and no innovation – if life were like this, we certainly would not be writing this book! These changes could be termed as variability and Frei (2006) suggests diagnosing the type of variability into the following categories:

- Arrival
- Request
- Capability
- Effort

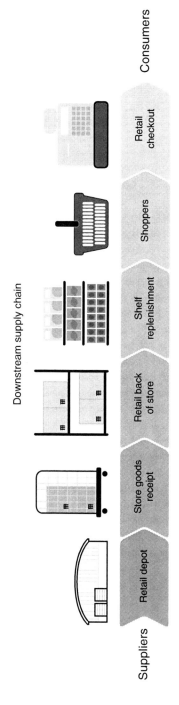

Fig. 10.2 Customers in the supply chain

Let's consider some examples in order to illustrate the concept when applied within a supply chain business.

Arrival variability is for example, when all orders to be picked in a warehouse supplying finished goods to a customer arrive mostly on a Friday afternoon. This occurs because the customer only processes the orders on a weekly fixed timetable. This results in the warehouse being quiet during the normally cheaper labour hire times of the week (Monday to Friday) and then very busy during the normally more expensive labour hire times of the weekend (Saturday and Sunday). The cost efficiency of the warehouse is affected by this variability.

An example of *request* variability is when a customer requests a differentiated service lead-time delivery; in other words, they might want a supplier to give them the option of a faster service than normal. This could be easy to execute, but for large organisations it will mean system changes, accounting changes, specialised assets and new staff training.

Capability variability is different again as this refers to the customer's ability to carry out tasks needed to receive service. For example, a manufacturer supplying to the retail trade may have some customers who are highly skilled in forecasting and demand planning, but others who are new to the subject. The manufacturer will need to consider this varying level of customer capability when inputting the forward forecast into their planning systems.

Effort variability is where the customer expends varying degrees of energy on tasks needed to receive service. For example, one retailer may put a lot of energy into shelf ready packaging, whereas another may not – causing a potential cost accounting difference which will need to be considered by a supplier.

Frei (2006) argues that each category needs to have a corresponding strategy that either accommodates or reduces the variability. Ideally these strategies ensure both a positive customer experience whilst still maintaining an efficient supply chain. Taking the arrival variability above, the warehouse may wish to provide a cost incentive if the customer orders mid week. This will help with their cost efficiency, and also enhances the customer experience by offering a cost discount. Likewise taking the capability example, the manufacturer could offer demand planning training to their customers. This would improve the efficiency of the input forecasts for the manufacture whilst importantly, enhancing the experience for the customer.

It is the pro-active engagement of customers with a strategy that offers real options against these different types of customer service variability that will drive successful customer relationships. This is a topic we are now going to consider further.

10.2 Managing Key Customers

Are all customers equal? Should we provide a better service to some than others? Following Pareto's law, which was introduced in Chap. 2 on Plan, our key customers generally make up only 20% of our total number of customers but contribute 80% of the turnover. Putting our energy into managing key customers and gaining loyalty is therefore critical for business success. Corporate organisations will normally prioritise their service towards customers who can create the most value for the organisation and high value customers are identified by assessing their lifetime value.

Key customers are those who are positively disposed to the organisation and thus easier to deal with. Servicing such customers becomes less costly with time and is summarised by the concept of "cost to serve". The concept of "cost to serve" is explained in detail by Christopher (2005). As well as being more profitable per unit delivered, key customers often function as what Reichheld calls "active promoters" – people providing positive, word-of-mouth advertising for the organisation (Reichheld 2003).

Typically, time is invested into segmenting customers into groups in order to define the service offer they should receive. In the B2C environment, this is seen very clearly with airlines who offer different targeted service levels depending on whether customers have a gold, silver or bronze status, for example. In supply chain companies the cost to serve is no different. Fast Moving Consumer Good (FMCG) companies operate a similar segmentation model where some customers enjoy a higher level of case fill than others.

To summarise, not all customers are equal. To give the same supply chain service to all customers means that our key customers would be under-served and our non-key customers, who give lower value, would be over-served. It is therefore important to understand the true lifetime value of a customer.

10.2.1   Customer Lifetime Value

A food retailer that spends €10,000 per week with a supplier is worth over €10 million in a relationship that lasts 20 years. This amount takes no account of other benefits such as contract growth, increased expenditure or the effects of highly satisfied customers acting as active promoters to other potential customers. The numbers explain the importance of developing successful, long-term relationships with our customers and this is called the customer lifetime value.

As a Harvard Business Review article concludes, "loyal" customer behaviours explain differences in companies' financial performance more than any other single factor. The author of the article also points out that customer satisfaction is the main driver for customer loyalty (Reichheld 2003).

There are other clear reasons for the importance of customer retention and for believing that customer retention is a better investment than customer acquisition. Research summarised by Edwards (2006) shows:

- Most of the cost of acquiring new customers occurs in the first year of the relationship, often before they actually become customers.

- As B2B customers stay, they tend to buy more of an organisation's products and services. The B2B organisation cross-sells as satisfied customers explore more of the organisation's product range.
- Long-term customers tend to be cheaper to service as their relationship with the organisation matures.
- Long-term customers are often prepared to pay a price premium.

10.2.2 Customer Service Ambassadors

To build relationships with our key customers we need employees who act as ambassadors both internally and externally; employees who think service-centrically and promote excellence in customer service in all actions that they carry out.

Organising employees in customer service teams has successfully supported the strategy of creating customer service ambassadors. The team structure has benefits like sharing the same objectives and having better knowledge of each others' job roles. This leads to increased involvement, job satisfaction and motivation with better communication between internal groups. Ultimately, there is more enjoyment working with others within the organisation and a higher likelihood of creating more customer service ambassadors.

Depending on the level of interaction with customers there are different soft skills requirements to become a customer service ambassador, for example listening skills. Being aware of your own emotions and those of your customers is very important and the area of emotional intelligence studies this. If we behave in an emotionally intelligent way we are better prepared to listen to customers, meet and exceed their expectations and deal with any problems effectively while maintaining a positive attitude. As discussed earlier, it is just as important to consider internal customers as well as external customers here. Developing customer service skills are a route to building customer service ambassadors. This can be achieved by:

- Recruiting new people with the required skills
- Redeploying people from one role to another
- Removing people who are unable to display the required skills
- Training and coaching people to improve their skills

Chapter 8 on People goes into more detail on how to build a learning and development strategy and link each employee's personal development plan to the company's goals.

10.3 Delivering Against Customer Needs

By measuring and managing customer expectations we are able to plan and implement customer service improvements. In many situations we work within contracts and service level agreements for internal and external customers.

By enhancing customer satisfaction when delivering our products and services, we can increase customer loyalty and generate repeat business.

We are now going to consider three elements for delivering against customer needs:

- Delivering the core promise
- Meeting and exceeding customer expectations
- Service recovery

10.3.1 Delivering the Core Promise

By working to agreed standards, suppliers and their customers can agree in principle the core service being offered prior to the service delivery. To help establish these customer expectations, it is normally considered best practice to set up a contract or Service Level Agreement (SLA). This SLA will state the key factors that are important for the relationship. These agreements contain measures or Key Performance Indicators (KPI) for services provided. An example of two key supply chain customer service KPI's are:

- Delivery On Time (OT)
- Delivery In Full (IF)

Delivery OT is calculated by agreeing a time (for example between 09:00 and 10:00) that the customer would like the delivery. During a month, if 100 deliveries are made and 5 of these deliveries miss this agreed time, then this would be calculated as 95/100 or 95% delivery OT.

Delivery IF measures the ability of a supplier to satisfy customer order quantity. During the same month, if 1,000 units are ordered and the supplier only delivers 900, then this would be calculated as 90% delivery IF.

The OT and IF measures are often combined within the supply chain, to make On Time In Full (OTIF). The combined measure in the above example would be $0.95 \times 0.90 = 0.855$ or 85.5% OTIF.

For internal measurement many organisations have followed the teachings of Kaplan and Norton (1996). For external measures a good source is given by the Supply Chain Council as introduced earlier in this guide (http://www.supply-chain.org). Both these works are recommendations for further reading.

10.3.2 Meeting and Exceeding Customer Expectations

As we saw from the service profit chain at the start of this chapter, external service value drives customer satisfaction, which in turn drives loyalty. Customer satisfaction is an evolving puzzle that needs to be continually solved. Essentially in every interaction we will have a moment of truth – where the customer judges their experience.

This judgement of service delivery can be made by the customer alone, as their perception of the experience is their reality. An element of our customer service delivery becomes almost intangible. We cannot see it, but our customers experience it. Kotler et al. (2008) state that if the product or service exceeds expectations, then the consumer is highly satisfied; if it falls short, the consumer is dissatisfied.

In B2B organisations within the supply chain, it is very likely that customers are served more than just once. Building an excellent customer service reputation that is founded on maintaining excellent customer satisfaction levels is very important. These relationships are founded, strengthened or indeed weakened by the perception of the service that customers receive. The strength of the relationship has a central role in influencing their buying behaviour in the future.

A number of factors determine the customer service perception. For example, the customers' previous experiences from other service encounters will influence their expectations for the future. They will also build their expectations through word-of-mouth communication from colleagues, friends and the media.

Customer satisfaction erodes over time, not because any physical decline occurs, but rather because there is a relative decline in performance perception of supply chain companies.

In principle, there are only two solutions to this dilemma:

- We can try to manage increasing customer expectations, so that they rise more slowly, or perhaps don't rise at all.
- We can improve our customer service much more rapidly and positively so that we at least keep pace with the demands of our customers.

To meet or exceed our customer's expectations we need to:

- Know our companies procedures
- Know our companies products and services
- Give correct information to our customers
- Emphasise the benefits of our products and services
- Communicate effectively
- Execute operations effectively

Part of meeting or exceeding customers' expectations requires supply chain companies to evolve with customers. As customers move into different geographical markets and use new technologies, it is important for a supply chain company to change with the customer, or risk being left behind. Organisations can improve their customer service offer, but customers' expectations can accelerate at an even faster rate. For example, TNT Express, the global logistics company, improved their service offer by announcing in 2010 they have put 12 Scania R-series trucks into their South East Asia road network. This, it is hoped, would enhance customer satisfaction. However this is not a certainty and consideration must be given to how this offer compares with rivals, such as FedEx, who offer a free of charge online shipping tool to manage international shipments.

In summary, it is up to everybody in the supply chain organisation to consider the expectations puzzle outlined above. It is the entire organisation's responsibility to meet and exceed expectations, much wider than simply the service personal that operate daily with customers.

10.3.3 Service Recovery

The National Complaints Culture Survey 2006 identifies the following key statistics regarding complaints and service recovery (Hicks 2006):

- 68% of consumers say they are willing to pay up to 20% more to stay with an organisation that offers exceptional service.
- 60% of consumers are willing to complain about products; 46% are prepared to make a complaint about services.
- Of customers who choose not to make a complaint, 33% of them say it is because they believe that the organisation "won't do anything about it".
- 94% of those complaining by email think their complaint should be dealt with within 1 week, but this happens in only 49% of cases.
- 89% of customers are more likely to tell others about bad service experiences; only 60% are likely to talk about good experiences.

In fact, one element that makes service great can be defined by how organisations deal with problems and complaints. Complaints can actually be good for an organisation. Edwards (2006) identifies that complaints enable customers to have their problems solved quickly and effectively. They also are critical to identifying and implementing improvements in the service as they are essentially free customer feedback. Finally and perhaps most importantly, customers whose problems have been dealt with well may well become loyal ambassadors for the organisation.

It is key for an organisation to have a clear service recovery process that is understood by all people within the business. This includes skills that need to be practice for managing service recovery, for example handling challenging situations with customers. Service recovery, rather than being used as a tool for blame, can be used to improve business processes and promote customer loyalty.

Let us go back to the start of this chapter where we considered the service profit chain. The starting point was to have effective operational processes. Ideally these would guide our employees to deliver great internal and external service in every customer interaction. However, in the event that customer satisfaction is not met, we need effective operational service recovery processes in order to loop us back onto the service profit chain. Ultimately, customer service exists for a reason: improved business performance.

10.4   Case Study of Best Practice in Customer Service: Unilever

Unilever South Africa: Winning in the marketplace through customer service

Recession, skyrocketing prices and economic downturn were the buzzwords of 2008. All we heard around us were stories of doom and gloom. Following a period of change and reorganisation in 2007, Unilever South Africa (ULSA) entered this phase of unpredictability and pessimism, faced with challenges in their customer service delivery.

The three previously separate Foods, Home & Personal Care and Ice Cream businesses were merged into One Unilever. The business was characterised by system integration challenges, high levels of employee turnover, skill and process erosion and loss of morale. The resultant approach to customer service became fire fighting – addressing symptoms of the customer service issues and not root causes. The problem boiled down to availability of products on shelf. If the products were not available on shelf when the shopper went to the store, no amount of marketing could make up for it.

Customer service KPI

Customer service in Unilever is measured using Customer Case Fill On Time (CCFOT): This measurement includes all service and efficiency losses from the point of original order that the customer places to the final receipt of the product by the customer. It is more rigorous than traditional Case Fill in that it includes measurement of efficiency loss and external losses (outside of Unilever's control). In 2008, ULSA's customer service as measured in CCFOT averaged 61% (with lowest point at 48%). This meant that out of 100 cases of product ordered, the customer would receive only 61 cases at the right time when the customer needed it.

Taking ownership

In order to improve their customer service, ULSA started with a deep understanding of the root cause behind poor service delivery. Customer service losses were analysed by a cross-functional team. The output indicated improvements required across people, systems and organisation. This supported the South African Board's drive for a more holistic and business wide approach to customer service. The resultant improvement programme therefore not only addressed the traditional areas like sourcing unit capacities, but also included system and business process improvements, people skills and capability, leadership and behavioural elements. The Board took ownership of the improvement programme, championing it through the business and driving strong KPI alignment behind CCFOT. CCFOT improvements were also written into the performance bonus targets across the business.

(continued)

Behavioural enablers

The behavioural enablers that were fundamental to the improvement programme were customer service mindset and new ways of working. It was evident that everybody within the company needed to own customer service, not only the supply chain function. To make service culture second nature both with internal and external customers, the service mindset training was driven across all functions throughout the business.

The team also encouraged the building of a culture of root causes analysis, as opposed to fire fighting, and continuous improvement throughout the organisation, not just in the manufacturing environment.

In the development and delivery of the improvement programme, the South African team drew heavily on the expertise, best practice and support of the regional Customer Service Excellence team.

Positive results

Keeping in mind the service profit chain model, every 3% of service improvement would equal 1% of growth for business. The overall aim of the customer service improvement programme was to lift customer service from the 2008 level of 61% to above 90% whilst reducing inventory as measured in days on hand to <60.

The successes of this major customer service improvement programme were already apparent: at the end of 2009 – about 1 year into the project – with an increased service level to about 85% in CCFOT and a 33% decrease in inventory, exiting below 60 days and releasing R650m cash for growth. This was delivered in parallel with a massive SC transformation project of combining and optimising the previously separate Foods and Home & Personal Care ambient distribution networks into one.

Outlook

Whilst the results so far have been impressive, much more needs to be done to ensure that ULSA's improved customer service will be maintained. The team is now focusing on embedding the gained improvements into the organisation.

Unilever South Africa aims to

- Ensure that improvements of 2009 are maintained in the face of market volatility and business complexities.
- The new ways of working and customer mindset to becomes a way to life in everyday work.
- Remain aligned to their customers, both internally and externally.

Through these three steps, the team is determined to continue its journey of winning in the marketplace through customer service.

Customer Service Team
Unilever South Africa

10.5   Suggestions for Further Reading

Blanchard, K. H., Ballard, J., Finch, F. (2004). *Customer mania: It's never too late to build a customer-focused company*. New York: Free Press.

Blanchard, K. H., & Bowles, S. M. (1993). *Raving fans: A revolutionary approach to customer service*. New York: William Morrow & Company.

Gattorna, J. L., & Friends (2009). *Dynamic supply chain alignment*. Farnham: Gower Publishing Ltd.

Johnston, R., & Clark, G. (2005). *Service operations management: Improving service delivery*. Upper Saddle River, NJ: Pearson Prentice Hall.

References

Christopher, M. (2005). *Logistics and supply chain management: creating value-added networks*. Financial Times Prentice Hall: Harlow.

Edwards, S. (2006). *Best practice guide for customer service professionals*. London: Customer 1st International.

Emmet, S. (2007). *The customer service toolkit*. Cirencester: Management Books 2000 Ltd.

Frei, F. X. (2006). Breaking the trade-off between efficiency and service. *Harvard Business Review, 84*(11), 92.

Heskett, J. L., & Sasser, W. E. (2010). The service profit chain: From satisfaction to ownership. In P. Maglio, C. Kieliszewski, & J. Spohrer (Eds.), *Handbook of service sciences* (pp. 19–29). New York: Springer Science+ Business Media.

Hicks, C. (2006). *National complaints culture survey*. Redditch: TMI.

Kaplan, R. S., & Norton, D. P. (1996). *The balanced scorecard: Translating strategy into action*. Cambridge, MA: Harvard Business School Press.

Kotler, P., Armstrong, G., & Cunningham, P. H. (2008). *Principles of marketing*. Pearson Prentice Hall: Upper Saddle River, NJ.

Reichheld, F. F. (2003). The one number you need to grow. *Harvard Business Review, 81*(12), 46–55.

Chapter 11
Guide to Outsourcing in Supply Chain Management

Abstract This chapter guides you through the topic of outsourcing in supply chain management. This chapter is structured as follows: first it considers the breadth, growth drivers and common reasons and concerns for outsourcing. Second, it will then define the tendering activities; where a nine-step process is highlighted. Third, it explains how service can be improved through better third party logistics management and the evolving future of outsourcing in the business world. This chapter will conclude with an overview on outsourcing trends.

Having read this chapter you will be able to:

- Demonstrate good practice of distribution outsourcing and the associated tendering process
- Assess operations in your company and decide whether outsourcing presents a viable option
- Recognise how improved service can be reached in your existing outsourcing relationships through better third party logistics management

11.1 What is Outsourcing?

Outsourcing has gained momentum recently and the trend is likely to continue for the coming decades. We can define outsourcing as the process of moving aspects of your own company to another supplier. In supply chain management, we speak about outsourcing when functions such as buying, manufacturing, warehousing and transportation are given to another supplier, referred to as the 3rd Party Logistics (3PL) provider.

Outsourcing is normally considered when your company doesn't have the capability to perform the specific task, or when your company believes that another organisation can perform the task better. In fact, businesses can outsource the majority of their supply chain activities if they wish. Companies such as Benetton or Nike tend to outsource their manufacturing, distribution and retailing, leaving them to focus on marketing their apparel products.

C. Scott et al., *Guide to Supply Chain Management*,   169
DOI 10.1007/978-3-642-17676-0_11, © Springer-Verlag Berlin Heidelberg 2011

This chapter will focus on outsourcing in distribution and logistics, in particular the outsourcing of transportation and warehousing services.

11.1.1   Growth Drivers in Outsourcing

What are the drivers for the increasing number of logistics processes being outsourced? We can identify that there are three main drivers:

- Globalisation
- Increasing complexity
- Emerging markets

3PLs know that global companies have global needs. At the same time they have realised that it's more difficult to operate in a global environment than just serving local markets. 3PLs have therefore expanded their services and offer fully integrated services in global transportation and distribution. Thus, *globalisation* and associated global needs is a key driver for the current growth in outsourcing.

The *increasing complexity* of supply chain management is closely linked to the globalisation of business. Global markets certainly offer a lot of advantages to many businesses, but they also have some downsides. Let's think about the complexity of multiple freight transport options for the distribution of finished goods. In order to reduce this complexity in-house, companies choose to outsource their logistics to 3PLs. These 3PL providers specialise in this area and it is their core competence.

The economic growth in the Far East, as well as in Eastern Europe, is the third driver for growth in logistics outsourcing. Just imagine what it means in terms of transportation volumes and warehousing space when companies realise double-digit growth in Russia for example? Thus, *emerging markets* drive logistics outsourcing.

11.1.2   Common Reasons for Outsourcing

The most common reasons for a supply chain to engage in outsourcing are:

- Increase operating flexibility
- Reduce fixed assets
- To increase efficiency

The first reason is to *increase operating flexibility*. If you don't own your primary and secondary transport, it's much easier for you to cope with seasonal swings (e.g. Easter or Christmas) or to switch between transportation modes (i.e. from rail to road transportation).

This might save you money as you do not need to provide transport capacity for all occasions and it definitely *reduces fixed assets*. 3PL service providers are specialists in what they do and you don't need to hold assets that are not part of the core business.

Thirdly, many companies want to reduce their operating costs. 3PLs aim to spend less while achieving better results. Thus, reduced operating costs leading to *increased efficiency* through logistics outsourcing is another common reason behind the decision to outsource.

11.1.3 Outsourcing Concerns

There are some concerns associated with outsourcing your logistics processes to a service provider. For example, outsourcing secondary transport to another company means losing the direct interface with the customer. This can mean that you have less customer contact and therefore lose control over the relationship.

Furthermore, 3PLs have great knowledge about their own business, but it needs time for them to get to know your business.

Another risk is that once a long-term contract is signed and a commitment made by both parties, the 3PL's customer mindset may diminish to be left with a logistics provider that is operating in a Business-to-Business (B2B) environment and loses the Business-to-Customer/Consumer (B2C) focus.

11.2 The Tendering Process of Outsourcing

The tendering process is a clearly defined process for contractor selection including all key steps from scoping of outsourcing requirements, through to the final negotiation and contract agreement (Rushton and Walker 2007). There are nine steps in the tendering process (see Fig. 11.1).

Let's take a closer look at each step within the tendering process from the perspective of the supply chain company wishing to outsource.

11.2.1 Step 1: Review Scope for Outsourcing and Requirements

The first step involves an internal assessment of the need for outsourcing. In this first step, it is important to reflect which processes within your company could be potential outsourcing candidates and whether outsourcing is the right step to be taken for these processes. Don't believe that outsourcing will heal any sick or poisoned logistics operations. We should remember that if we outsource a mess, all we will get back is a different mess.

As there are various types of operations to be outsourced, you also need to decide which mode of operation you want to go for: dedicated or shared resources.

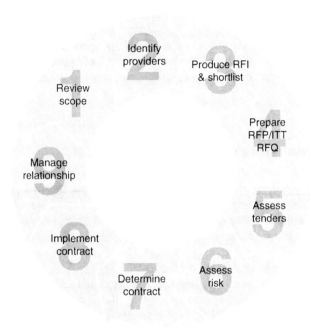

Fig. 11.1 Nine tendering process steps adapted from Rushton and Walker (2007)

Dedicated resources mean that a 3PL provides a complete logistics or distribution operation to one of its clients exclusively.

Shared resources are logistics services that a 3PL may offer to multiple clients in the same operation. For example, various customers might use a distribution centre if similarity of product characteristics allows. Another reason behind a shared resource option might be excess capacity: in which case, one company's volume is not enough to operate the resource at full capacity, so another smaller customer is taken on board.

Figure 11.2 shows some advantages and disadvantages of each mode of operation.

Exclusiveness and an assurance of confidentiality are two of the advantages to be gain when deciding for a *dedicated* operation. On the other hand, these might come at a total higher cost due to underutilisation during seasonal swings.

Shared resources, in contrast, will benefit from economies of scale and therefore will be able to maximise asset utilisation resulting in lower unit cost. The downside of shared operations may be conflicting demands and less expertise and specialisation for your business.

Some of these questions will help you in choosing the right mode of transportation:

- Which geographical factors do I have to consider?
- What are the transport implications when choosing dedicated versus shared?

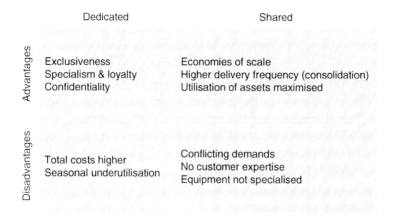

	Dedicated	Shared
Advantages	Exclusiveness Specialism & loyalty Confidentiality	Economies of scale Higher delivery frequency (consolidation) Utilisation of assets maximised
Disadvantages	Total costs higher Seasonal underutilisation	Conflicting demands No customer expertise Equipment not specialised

Fig. 11.2 Dedicated or shared resources adapted from Rushton and Walker (2007)

- What are the implications for security and confidentiality?
- How does the decision impact my company's service and cost targets?
- Would a hybrid solution, thus a mixture of shared and dedicated resources, be feasible?

If you are undecided, you can keep both options open and ask the service providers to quote on basis of both: the dedicated and the shared operation.

11.2.2 Step 2: Identify Potential Service Providers

The next step in the tendering process is to draw up a *long list* of potential service providers. This part can be quite difficult as there are plenty of service providers in the marketplace.

Here are some useful questions that might help you in the identification process. You could, for example, check whether the 3PL has invested in:

- IT equipment, including online links and tracking equipment?
- Human resources, e.g. staff training?
- Resources and facilities to meet specific requirements?
- Infrastructure, including network coverage, fleet and depots?

Furthermore, there are other items that will affect the outsourcing decision, e.g. the provider's ability to provide:

- A complete logistics package
- Quality of service
- Reliability in performance
- Access to top management
- Strong partnerships
- Implementation record

11.2.3   Step 3: Produce Request for Information and Shortlist

We have just identified our long list, now it's time to contact each potential service provider and ask for specific information. You can do this by sending a Request For Information (RFI) document to all potential providers on your list.

The aim of doing so is twofold. Firstly, you want to ensure that the 3PL is interested in tendering for the business and secondly, you want to check again whether you believe the 3PL would be suitable for the tender.

Let's now have a look at the contents of the RFI. The RFI is a concise document covering different key areas of information:

1. Introduction and confidentiality clause
2. Description of your company
3. Description of the opportunity:

   • What does your company wish to outsource?
   • Does your company have any preference for dedicated or shared resources?

4. The selection process (e.g. timescale and key selection criteria)
5. Response:

   • What contents does the service provider have to submit in order to respond to the RFI?
   • In what format should the 3PL submit the data?

Once you have received back responses to your RFI, you can evaluate those based on your key selection criteria that you will previously have defined. As a result of this process step, you should be left with five to ten contractors for tender.

11.2.4   Step 4: Prepare and Issue the Request for Quotation

A Request For Quotation (RFQ) is an extensive yet important document. Its purpose is to collect detailed data and information from the short-listed companies in a standard format. An Invitation To Tender (ITT) and Request For Proposal (RFP) are synonyms to the RFQ.

You might ask yourself why it is important to create another document. The collection of further data in a standardised format is crucial to ensure consistency and comparability of information to facilitate your selection process. Later, during the assessment phase, you need comparable information to make your selection; a standard response format will ease the process of comparison. Typically, an RFQ will include the following sections:

• Business description and background
• Data provided with the RFI
• Physical distribution network

- Information systems
- Distribution service levels and performance monitoring
- Risk assessment
- Industrial and business relations
- Charging structure
- Terms and conditions
- The selection procedure and response format including deadlines

An example for a section in an RFQ concerning the charging structure for distribution costs can be found in Fig. 11.3.

After having sent the RFQ and received the data back from potential contractors, we can proceed to the next step in the outsourcing process.

11.2.5 Step 5: Assess the Tenders

For this step, you need some time for assessment, reflection and discussion. This can best be done in cross-functional teams. For distribution outsourcing the people involved in these teams are likely to be Logistics, Procurement, Finance and Human Resources. The latter often need to be involved, as outsourcing will most likely result in internal personnel changes.

11.2.6 Step 6: Select Contract and Assess Risk

The contract selection itself is now a fairly straightforward task; you will have put a lot of effort in the structured approach for gathering information and assessing the tenders. A visit to the most favoured 3PLs is a good way to get to know the reference sites further and to engage with the onsite management.

At this stage, you could make a risk assessment to identify any factors that might be an issue for the contract implementation or the outsourced operations. Examples for areas of risk are:

- Operational/service risk: Sudden demand changes, new product introduction, information system failure
- Business risk: 3PLs insolvency, tax problems
- External risk: Fire or flooding

11.2.7 Step 7: Determine Contract

The final contract has to be formulated and agreed at this step. The contract contains a large amount of detailed information and requirements. Contracts differ from company to company, but should contain these three key areas: object, cost and service. Here are some examples for each of the cost elements:

Transport	3PL Supplier Charges ('000s)				
	Year 1	Year 2	Year 3	Year 4	Year 5
Fuel	700	700	800	800	900
Tyres	100	100	100	100	100
Normal maintenance	200	250	300	350	400
Accident damage	50	50	50	50	50
Short-term hired equipment	60	60	60	60	60
3PL management fee	2	2	2	2	2
Total variable vehicle costs	1,112	1,162	1,312	1,362	1,512

Fig. 11.3 Example transport charging structure in RFQ

- *Object* related factors: warehouses, equipment, personnel
- *Cost* related factors: capital investments, operational and management costs
- *Service* related factors: service level agreement

For further information on contract creation, you can consult the Chartered Institute of Logistics and Transport (CILT) webpage, where you can find a blank contract with some guidelines (http://www.ciltuk.org.uk).

11.2.8   Step 8: Implement Contract

Many companies experience problems with the implementation of the outsourcing contract to an external supplier. One reason behind the troublesome implementation phase might be that there is no project management applied to that phase.

It is essential that the outsourcing company set up an implementation plan that defines the tasks for both the company as well as the contractor that includes some contingency planning. The implementation thus needs to be planned carefully and a back-up plan for each outsourced process should be available. By providing these steps your company can minimise the risk of an unsatisfactory outsourcing relationship.

11.2.9   Step 9: Manage Ongoing Relationship

Once the contract has been implemented, the challenge is to manage the ongoing relationship and thereby improve service. This is discussed in the next part of this chapter.

11.3   Improved Service Through Better 3PL Management

The first part of this chapter explained the tendering process for outsourcing and its associated nine steps. This part will have been especially important for someone engaging in logistics outsourcing. For companies with outsourcing experience – whether this experience has been particularly positive or negative – the second part of this chapter will be of great relevance.

So, assuming that you have been involved in outsourcing relationships already, how can we make the 3PL relationship better? The first step is to understand the motivation of the contractor. Do you know the motivation of your contractor? Does he want to fight or is he interested in a win-win? If you both want to win in that outsourcing relationship, it is best to be open and make this shared goal transparent to each other. This way, you can gain most out of the situation. But if you are not sharing your goals and strategies, this is likely to have a negative impact on your business. Furthermore, you can easily fall into a trap where in the end both parties involved lose.

11.3.1 Disputes: Why Outsourcing Relationships Fail

We mostly learn about success stories – examples where the outsourcing relationship worked and all parties involved were satisfied. However, real life shows that many partnerships and outsourcing contracts fail or end in a dispute.

What might be the reasons behind a failing outsourcing relationship? The reasons behind a failing outsourcing relationship are varied and the responsibility may be attributed to the 3PL, the outsourcing company or both (Rushton and Walker 2007).

Reasons why the 3PL might be responsible:

- Too little involvement and pushing back during negotiation, design and implementation phase
- Over-promising on capabilities of 3PL
- Unclear about customer requirements
- Poor implementation on 3PL side
- No continuous improvement
- Poor service levels and performance
- Not behaving as part of the customer's supply chain

Reasons why the outsourcing company might be responsible:

- Inaccurate volume information from customer (too low or too high)
- Inappropriate resources to manage 3PL
- Unclear or unrealistic expectation on outcome
- Poor outsourcing contract implementation on customer side
- Cost reduction focus too strong
- No clear SLA in place
- 3PL regarded just as another supplier

Reasons why both might be responsible:

- Unclear contract
- No clear goal setting and performance measurement
- Poor implementation
- Poor communication

11.3.2 Managing Expectations

In order to ensure success in outsourced relationships, we need to actively manage the relationship from start to finish.

Your company, as it engages in an outsourcing relationship, will have certain expectations towards a 3PL service provider. You might, for example, expect that a supplier provides superior service and execution while showing trust, openness and information sharing behaviour to you and your colleagues. You might also expect frequent solution innovations as well as additional service offerings matching your internal strategy.

On the other hand, the logistics service provider will have expectations of you as well. A contractor will probably expect that the outsourcing relationship will be mutually beneficial and long-term, and that prices are agreed on a fair basis. Moreover, the contractor might also expect trust, openness and information sharing from you, and will rely on the provision of clear service level agreements.

What happens if expectations are not formulated and shared between the two parties involved? Customers and contractors will not be fully satisfied. They will think that the other party could do more or something different to make the outsourcing relationship successful. Therefore, it's important that expectations are shared and that both parties work towards the same goals.

11.3.3   Managing the Relationship

It is now clear why we need to manage the outsourcing relationship. We are aware that there is some need for it. However, we don't know yet how we will actually execute the management of it. Ultimately, we need to go back to the start of this chapter and ask ourselves: How do we best improve our service through better 3PL management?

The two key areas for management are performance monitoring and operational control.

11.3.3.1   Performance Monitoring

There are two fundamental characters in 3PL performance monitoring: checking agreed service levels and monitoring that services are delivered at acceptable cost. Therefore, you need to monitor the operations and their performance. Performance can be monitored through financial measures or customer service measures. Further performance KPIs measuring internal processes or innovation and learning can be added.

A standardised format to set targets and review performance is the SLA between you and the contractor.

In order to monitor performance, you have to set targets for your customer service level, delivery time and order-picking accuracy performance indicators. In doing so, you can use historical data, budget constraints or industry standards, if available, as benchmarks.

11.3.3.2   Operational Control

Performance measures and monitors now need to be translated into a rolling operational plan. In an operational plan, costs are divided by period (week or month), by functional element (fuel or insurance), by logistics component (transport or warehousing) and by activity (customer or product group).

Once you have implemented the operational plan, and have monitored the measures for a number of periods, you may find deviations between actual and targeted performance measures. Three major causes of deviation are:

1. Changes in the level of activity, e.g. less work available on equipment
2. Changes in efficiency or performance, e.g. more downtimes on machines than planned
3. Changes in price, e.g. cost of fuel has increased

Depending on the magnitude of the deviations, you might have to agree other targets or, in cases of very drastic and enduring changes, you may have to rethink the outsourcing relationship and restart the tendering process.

In conclusion, outsourcing in supply chain management has experienced some steady growth as global manufacturing companies focus more on their core capabilities, such as product development, and hand over parts of their operational processes to external companies that are specialists in that field. Logistics outsourcing, therefore, can be defined as the contracting of transport and warehousing to a 3PL provider. The nine-step tendering process supports the company that wants to outsource in identifying outsourcing need, inviting external companies for tender and selecting a contractor.

However, there is also a risk associated with logistics outsourcing: the relationship might end in a dispute and subsequently fail before the termination of the contract. Therefore, the management of expectations as well as active performance monitoring and operational control are essential in achieving improved service and successful logistics outsourcing.

11.4   Case Study of Best Practice in Outsourcing: Hi-Tech Industry

3PL trends from the hi-tech and electronics industry

According to a global research study conducted in 2006, about 80% of international manufacturing companies are involved in logistics outsourcing (Langley et al. 2006). In this industry, analysts see a growth of 20% year by year; companies are outsourcing more and more services to 3PLs.

(continued)

Let's take a look at Cisco Systems, the global player in the semi-conductors industry. Cisco Systems decided to completely outsource all logistics flows in Europe, Middle East and North America to UPS Logistics as a 4PL^{TM} (van Hoek 2004). This means that UPS now co-ordinates and manages all supplier and customer facing logistics activities. This is done by both using the UPS transport and warehousing network or by tendering processes out to other logistics providers.

The inbound process between UPS and Cisco System works as follows: once the products are ready for shipment, UPS is notified. UPS then collects the goods within 24 h. Next, the logistics provider books an aircraft to bring the goods onto the continent. UPS has built a European logistics centre of 86,000 square feet, owned and operated by them, but fully dedicated to Cisco's products.

On the outbound side, the customer places an order, which triggers UPS to select a carrier. UPS uses various carrier algorithms based on service level, price and in-transit time. Every time a carrier is selected, a mini RFQ is issued to a list of approved carriers. Then, shipments with a common destination are consolidated.

UPS ensures full system integration and transparency: the order status is always available and customers can change delivery dates up until shortly before order fulfilment.

In summary, Cisco Systems have benefited a lot from this outsourcing of logistics processes. The staggering fact is that UPS now handles more than one million boxes for Cisco annually.

Despite the recent economic downturn, supply chain executives in the hi-tech and electronics industries remain positive about their outsourcing commitments. A recent industry report indicates, that 55% of hi-tech shippers expect that they will be able to keep freight rates at the reduced level they negotiated during the recession (Eyefortransport 2010). However, only 14% of 3PLs expect that they will be able to continue offering these reduced rates. Thus, there is a disconnect between the rate expectations of companies like Cisco and the outsourcing solution cost that 3PLs are willing to offer.

Overall, the hi-tech industry seems optimistic about the coming years with 37% of supply chain executives stating that their industry's performance had been better than other industries in the recession.

11.5   Suggestions for Further Reading

Rushton, A., & Walker, S. (2007). *International logistics and supply chain outsourcing: From local to global*. London: Kogan Page Ltd.

References

Eyefortransport (2010). *2010 Hi-tech & electronics supply chain report*. 5th Hi-Tech and Electronics Supply Chain Summit, Amsterdam: Eyefortransport.

Langley, C. J., Dort, E. V., Topp, U., & Sykes, S. R. (2006). *Third-party logistics: Results and findings of the 11th annual study*. Atlanta, GA: Georgia Institute of Technology, Capgemini, DHL and SAP.

Rushton, A., & Walker, S. (2007). *International logistics and supply chain outsourcing: from local to global*. London: Kogan Page Ltd.

van Hoek, R. I. (2004). UPS logistics and to move towards 4PL – or not? Transportation and Logistics Educators Conference, Philadelphia, PA

About the Authors

Colin Scott

Colin is an author and executive coach for global companies with over 20 years of experience in business and supply chain management. In his operational career, he worked for manufacturers and third-party logistics providers and managed major change projects, building new distribution centres as well as moving and consolidating depots. He was responsible for international transport operations as well as systems strategy and implementation and held Commercial Manager positions, focusing on customer account management and regional financial responsibility, including the management of client inventory and the implementation of strategic sourcing processes.

Over the past decade, Colin has focused on management development, designing and delivering learning programs around the globe for some of the world's largest companies. He thoroughly enjoys supporting large retailers, manufacturers, transportation and logistics companies in meeting the ever-increasing challenges in customer service, cost, innovation and the environment.

Educated at Durham University and Nottingham Business School, Colin holds diplomas in logistics and management studies and is an accredited trainer and assessor in Team Management Profiling. A passionate sports player, Colin believes in a strong link between sports and business – high performance is created by knowledge, skills and attitude through coaching and learning.

Henriette Lundgren

Henriette is an author, coach and business trainer. Her main focus is on developing and conducting supply chain, demand planning and customer service trainings for leading multinational companies. Before joining the world of HR development, she worked for more than 6 years in various line management and project management positions in the supply chain industry, leading demand planning and sourcing teams in the consumer goods and chemical industry. She also oversaw the implementation of SAP systems in manufacturing, planning and customer service at the international level.

Henriette holds a degree in International Business from Maastricht University (NL) and a Master in Organizational Psychology from the Open University in

C. Scott et al., *Guide to Supply Chain Management*,
DOI 10.1007/978-3-642-17676-0, © Springer-Verlag Berlin Heidelberg 2011

Germany. She also received a Professional Diploma from the Chartered Institute of Logistics and Transportation (CILT) with distinction and is a member of the British Psychological Society (BPS).

Henriette has worked and lived in various countries, including Italy, Poland, Sweden, Germany and the Netherlands, which makes her a true and multilingual European citizen. In her free time, Henriette enjoys baking cakes.

Paul Thompson

Paul is an author and business learning specialist with extensive experience in designing and running global programmes for large corporations. He enjoys working with leading companies and has developed and delivered coached learning activities in topical subjects, including customer service, supply chain and value creation. Many of Paul's programmes include the use of business simulations, which improve interaction during the event and increase learning transfer after it. He is a qualified assessor for the Margerison–McCann Team Management Wheel.

After graduating with a first class degree in Manufacturing Sciences, Paul spent a decade managing different parts of the business for two of the world's largest and most successful companies. In his roles, Paul has managed Sales, Finance, Planning, Supply Chain, Logistics, Warehousing and Manufacturing Operations.

He has led major change management projects including outsourcing international warehousing & distribution and implementing customer service excellence systems. In addition, he also oversaw the implementation of both SAP and JD Edwards successfully within the supply chain.

Index

Lightning Source UK Ltd.
Milton Keynes UK
UKOW031501121212

203572UK00001B/87/P